CRACOW

A TREASURY OF POLISH CULTURE AND ART

Michał Rożek

translated by Doris Ronowicz

Interpress Publishers, Warsaw

Graphic layout by
Jerzy Kępkiewicz

Production editor:
Wiesław Pyszka

Colour photographs by
Jan Popłoński

On the jacket photo by Jan Morek

Photographs by Jan Rosikoń on p. 133 (top) and 154 and Monika Krajewska on p. 140

Black-and-white photographs by Archiwum Polskiej Agencji Interpress

This is the two thousand two hundred and forty-fifth publication by Interpress

This book appears also in Polish, French and German

ISBN 83-223-2245-3

Prasowe Zakłady Graficzne — Wrocław, ul. P. Skargi 3/5

CONTENTS

1

2

3

5

4

6

7

9 11

8

10

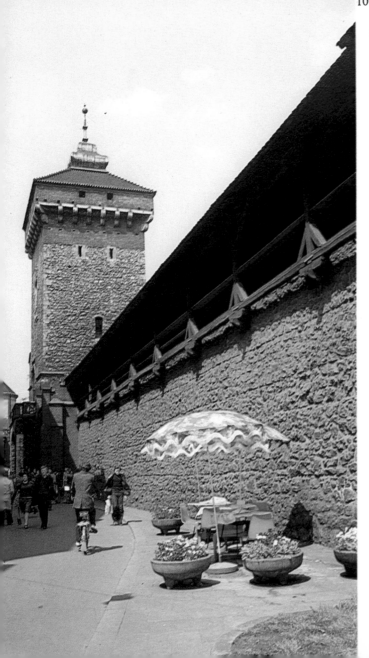

12   13   14

16

15   18

17

19

20 21

22

23

24

25

26

27

28

34

35

36

37

38

39

40

42

43

41

44

INTRODUCTION

In 1619, a panoramic copper-plate of Cracow, the work of Matthew Merian, left the Amsterdam printing house of Justus Hondius. It had the following significant inscription: *Cracovia totius Poloniae urbs celeberrima atque amplissima Regia, atque Academia insignis.* This is the way Cracow was described in the early 17th century. It was then a big metropolis with a large population and with wealth gathered over the centuries. The beauty of its magnificent buildings and its history as the former capital of Poland, made the city widely known and a favourite with foreigners, who liked to visit it in the past and still do today. The works of art gathered there are a glorious testimony to Polish artistic culture, bringing fame to both the artists and their sponsors. Today, Cracow is the seat of the voivodship authorities, a Roman Catholic Archbishopric, an important scientific and cultural centre and a centre of industry too. The coat of arms of the city is a blue shield on which there is a gate with three towers and in the centre of the middle tower there is a white eagle wearing a crown. The banner of Cracow is sky blue and white.

The culture of Cracow, the treasures of art kept in this city which is imbued with history, will be the subject of the further chapters of this book. The art of Cracow can without any exaggeration be treated as *pro toto* Polish art, for the majority of artistic phenomena had their beginnings there. It was the capital of the Polish state, later the place where kings were crowned and laid to rest, it is full of innumerable treasures of national culture, the seat of the oldest university in Poland. And finally it is the city that gave us the first Slav Pope — John Paul II.

What was and what is the role of Cracow in the culture of the Polish nation?

From the earliest ages the city took the lead in Poland as regards politics and culture. It was the seat of the rulers as early as the 11th century and the role of Cracow as capital was confirmed at the beginning of the 14th century. The historical central part of Cracow was shaped over a thousand years and it is one of the most artistically interesting town centres in Europe. Almost all artistic epochs left their mark on Cracow. It was here that the royal castle was built, as well as the cathedral where the monarchs of Poland were crowned and buried. From the Middle Ages, Cracow took a leading place in shaping Poland's culture. At the court of the duke a chancery was set up and there also the first Polish chronicle was written. A school and a library were set up in association with the Cathedral. In the Cathedral Treasury the royal crowns were carefully guarded. There are the best examples of Romanesque and Gothic art in Cracow. In the Middle Ages it was the scene of the development of literature and music. When the city became the place where coronations took place (1320) and also the place of residence of the ruler, the court culture radiated from Cracow to the provinces. Cracow University attracted students from the whole of Europe. The arts flourished.

It was the same in the 16th century. In the Renaissance period Cracow was the main centre of literary culture and a real home of the arts. Royal patronage and also that of the burghers operated widely.

The year 1609 marked a turning point in the history of the city. This was the year when the royal court moved out of Cracow. But the city retained the privileges of the capital — it remained the place of the coronations and burials of kings. This was observed faithfully in the Commonwealth of the Gentry. After this came a no less essential function — Cracow became a sanctuary of the life of the nation. In these years, certainly not the best in the history of Poland, years full of wars and violence, Cracow grew into a symbol of the good moments in the history of the nation. It had witnessed elevated moments in the times of the Piasts and Jagiellons. This state of affairs lasted till the end of the 18th century.

During the partitions of Poland, Cracow, entwined with the legend of history, fulfilled an important role in spreading and maintaining national consciousness. The walls, the stones spoke of the past, the good old days when everything was excellent and worth remembering. More than that — they taught history, they gave people a chance of national identification, they jolted the consciences of the Poles. This complex and perhaps rather pompous symbolism will only be understood by a nation that, if only for a few years, has experienced a loss of freedom. In the 19th century the old traditions were revived and from that time were cultivated solicitously. In the royal tombs, the spiritual leaders of the nation were laid to rest instead of kings. Great care was taken of historical monuments, which were regarded as a token of national identity. The Jagiellonian University was famed for its high standards of scholarship. Poles from all three sectors of partitioned Poland were educated there. The Academy of Learning, then called into being, integrated Poles from all over the country and provided a possibility of wide foreign contacts. Art and literature flourished, making Cracow the first of all the cultural centres of Poland at the beginning of the 20th century. It also had the honour of mobilizing the Polish troops during the First World War. The Polish Legions marched out of Cracow to do battle.

After independence had been regained, Cracow still remained the spiritual capital of Poland. The old, royal, Cracow shared all the good and bad moments with the rest of Poland. This specific combination gives Cracow its unique character — a symbol of Poland.

Today, Cracow impresses the wisitor with its magnificent collections of art and its many historic buildings. It is also one of the main centres of learning. The invaluable Cracow of today has inherited the wonderful atmosphere of the past, a charm you simply cannot resist, combined with a picturesqueness, that really cannot be described. It is a wonderful city, built to meet man's needs, with romantic little alleys, winding streets full of old buildings and beautiful churches. All the styles you could possibly think of, beginning with Romanesque and ending with *fin de siècle* and modern buildings, are to be found in Cracow.

This picture of Cracow would be incomplete without the legends and traditions associated with the city. They have defeated time and have remained alive to this very day, fascinating us with their vitality, although the beginnings of some of them are buried deep in the past.

Apart from the cultivation of the traditions, modern Cracow as a centre of artistic life is also famed for a few events of Europe-wide impact. Cracow is the place where the International Biennale of Graphic Art is held, as well as the Folk Art Fair and the Festival of Short Films. These events have already won world fame. In addition, for several years now, organ music festivals have been organized.

What are Cracow's prospects? The election of a Polish Pope, and UNESCO's decision to add Cracow to the list of cities of the world's cultural heritage, are undoubtedly the most important events in Cracow's recent history. Both of these historical facts put Cracow under an obligation. The city now confronts new and important changes, and the process of renewal has mapped out its development over the next several dozen years. Cracow must be saved from the threat of biological pollution to its natural environment. The invaluable treasures of world culture, which have survived there, must be preserved for future generations.

For Cracow makes people understand the values created by the nation over past centuries. The values of Cracow are lasting and this accounts for the national importance of the city and the care given to the restoration and preservation of its historic buildings, which we not only admire, but can also learn something from. Pope John Paul II, ending his pilgrimage to his native land, spoke these words at Cracow airport on 10 June 1979:

"I say farewell to Cracow, I wish the city a new youth, I wish that it may continue to be for the Poles, for Europe and the world, an excellent testimony to the history of the nation and the Church, and that the heritage of culture expressed in the walls of Cracow... should continue to speak its unique message."

CHAPTER I · IN THE DEPTHS OF EARLY MEDIAEVAL TIMES
(till the mid-13th century)

TOPOGRAPHY

Three geographical zones meet at the point where Cracow is situated: in the middle there is the Vistula Lowland, to the south the Carpathian Foothills, and to the north the Upland of Little Poland. The Vistula also flows through the middle of the city, with its tributaries (Rudawa, Wilga, Prądnik) which from the earliest times have facilitated communication. In the overflow arms of the Vistula, in the dry places, man built his settlements. Over these settlements towered Wawel Hill, formed of Jurassic limestone. In the opinion of a 16th century chronicler Marcin Bielski, "Cracow is situated in a very defendable place, on a plain, between swamps, the only access to it being through Kleparz, where the waters are very deceptive. When you look at it from the top of Zwierzyniec Hill (because that is where you get the best view) it looks rather like a lute, so roundly formed, and Grodzka Street with the castle is like the fingerboard of a lute. It is also rather like an eagle, whose head is the castle, Grodzka Street the neck, and the suburbs round the city the wings".

Cracow is situated 219 m. above sea level, exactly at the place where parallel 50 crosses meridian 20 to the east of Greenwich. That area has always enjoyed fertile land and rich natural resources. Rock salt has been mined to the east of Cracow, at Wieliczka and Bochnia. Lead, silver and zinc ores have been mined to the north-west of the city, near Olkusz. Near Swoszowice there are sulphur deposits. The forests surrounding Cracow supplied timber for fuel and building, animals for food, and were also a place of refuge if danger threatened. The limestone rocks, characteristic of the Upland of Little Poland, supplied a lasting building material. Fortified settlements were also built on them. These very good geographical conditions were the reason why Cracow developed so well. The hunter, farmer and shepherd were able to earn a good living here a thousand years ago. And, lastly, from the earliest times trade routes, going from Russia to Bohemia and from Hungary to the Baltic, crossed in Cracow, and were the main reason for the development of handicrafts and international trade.

THE ARCHAEOLOGICAL PAST

Before there were written sources, archaeological materials give us an idea of the oldest settlements in the area of the present city of Cracow. There is no information about the beginnings of the former capital of Poland in chronicles. A mediaeval legend tells us that the town was founded by Duke Krak, who defeated the terrible dragon living in the big cave under Wawel Hill. Bielski wrote that "under Wawel Hill there was a great dragon that ate three livestock at once and also stole people and their belongings and ate them, so they had to give him provender, in the form of three calves or sheep. So Krak told them to stuff sulphur into the skin of a calf and put it outside the dragon's cave in the morning. This was after he had spoken to Skuba, a cobbler, whom he afterwards rewarded richly. The dragon, coming out of his cave, ate the calf he found outside. But when he found that he couldn't swallow it, he drank water until he fell dead. One can still see his cave under the castle. It is called the Dragon's Cave". The daughter of Krak was the legendary Wanda, so well loved by the people. She took her own life by jumping into the Vistula. The mounds, which still stand today near Cracow, and have aroused the interest of researchers, are considered to be the tombs of Krak and Wanda. Those are the legends. There has been no explanation other than this of these prehistoric monuments. Perhaps they were symbolical tombs, which is the version accepted by tradition, or perhaps they were the guarding posts, or perhaps solar symbols.

The name Cracow (in Polish, *Kraków*) has a general Slavonic sound about it and is simply the genetive of Krak, which means that it belonged to him. There is no doubt about the fact that it originated from the man who bore the name of Krak, who was the founder of the town.

On the other hand, in the light of archaeological material we can say that the area of present-day Cracow always attracted man, from the very oldest times. Man settled there in the Palaeolithic Age, that is over 50,000 years B.C. He still led a nomadic life then. It was only in the Neolithic Age that he began to live around Wawel Hill permanently. Numerous excavations testify to this, including also cremation cemeteries. About 1300 B.C. there were quite dense settlements of people of the Lusatian culture, who are generally regarded by archaeologists as a proto-Slavic people. The Lusatian culture later developed into the Wend (Veneti) culture, which was a culture of the Slavic tribes, well known to Roman writers (Gaius Plinius Caecilius Secundus — Pliny the Younger, Cornelius Nepos, Cornelius Tacitus. Claudius Ptolemaeus). Rich finds representing this culture have been uncovered, including the *Dymarki*, that is, the metallurgical furnaces that prove the high level of technology reached by these people. There was also a large import of articles from the Roman empire, indicating the lively trade contacts of Rome with the Slav countries.

The end to the flourishing development of this vital culture was due to the migration of nations, and later the migration of Slav tribes from the upper Vistula.

In the 8th century, a defence castle was built on Wawel Hill to guard the surrounding settlements.

Scholars link it with the tribe of the Vislanes (Wiślanie). Relatively numerous mentions of this tribe are to be found in foreign chronicles. It was mentioned by the man who was known as the Bavarian Geographer in the middle of the 9th century, and a little later by the Anglo-Saxon King Alfred. The tribe already enjoyed some form of political organization. As early as the end of the 9th century, we can speak of the state of the Vislanes. Many scholars are of the opinion that its capital was Cracow. At any rate we know that the Vislane Duke, who is mentioned in *The Life of Methodius*, a source from the end of the 9th century. "a strong pagan prince, residing on the Wisła [Vistula], harassed many Christians and did them harm". Methodius therefore sent envoys to him and bade them say, "My son, it would be good for you to baptize yourself of your own free will in your own land, lest you be baptized by force in captivity in a foreign land; and you shall remember me". And the chronicler adds, "And this is what happened". The Slavonic rite, proclaimed by St. Methodius, the apostle to the Slavs, reached the Vistula from the Great Moravian State. But it was not long before Little Poland and Cracow learnt the Roman rite of Christianity, which replaced the liturgy in Slavonic language. After the fall of the Great Moravian State (906) the Vislanes regained political independence. But not for long. Soon after, neighbouring Bohemia had a loose superior authority over them, which brought the next, third, wave of Christianity and this time it came to stay. It is worth mentioning here, that the first Polish historical prince — Mieszko I — was christened only in 966, when the southern outskirts of Poland had been Christianized for quite some time already, although they did not yet belong to the lands ruled by the first Piast.

CRACOW IN THE DAYS OF THE FIRST PIASTS

The first pieces of information contained in written sources put an end to obscure theories and hypotheses concerning the beginnings of Cracow. The oldest of these is an account from the years 965/966 by Ibrahim ibn Jakub, a Spanish Jew in the service of the Arabs, who was travelling from distant Tortosa to Magdeburg, via Cracow, "Concerning the land of Bojeslaw [Boleslav I, Duke of Bohemia], the distance from Farago [Prague] to the city of Karako [Cracow] takes three weeks". From his further remarks we gather that: to Prague "Ruthenians and Slavs come from the city of Karako [Cracow] with goods". Poland, according to Ibrahim ibn Jakub "is abundant in food, meat, honey, and products of the fields". Cracow was then on a trade route, and Slav trade "reaches Russia and Constantinople by land and by sea". Thanks to these accounts of Ibrahim, Cracow entered the pages of history.

Whether Cracow was under a Bohemian duke or a Polish ruler in the middle of the 10th century is difficult to say today. In the opinion of many scholars, the so-called "Cracow State" was only attained by Mieszko after 977, that is, following the death of his wife, Dobrava, who was the daughter of the Bohemian Duke Boleslav I and the mother of King Boleslaus the Brave. And it is very probable that Mieszko took Cracow for his first-born son Boleslaus and began to rule there in the year 981, and — during his lifetime — gave "the Cracow State", as a separate district of Poland, to Boleslaus the Brave. The other lands were to be inherited by the sons of Oda, the second wife of Mieszko I (d. 992). So young Boleslaus the Brave settled in Cracow. He used his power to concentrate suitable material and military means to carry out his ambitious political plans. His father, Mieszko I, died in 992, and after his death Boleslaus mastered the rest of Poland by force, concentrating power in his own hands. He removed his younger brothers from the government and united the whole state under his sceptre. The year 992 was therefore the year of the birth of the Polish State in the true sense of the word. The fact that Boleslaus lived in Cracow for a number of years made it the leading capital city of all those in the Polish State of those days.

It is not out of the question that Cracow gained a missionary bishopric in the second half of the 10th century, with which Prochor and Prokulf, two enigmatic bishops, were linked before the year 1000. Their names were written in the oldest Register of Cracow Bishops. The Cracow bishopric was attached to the Gniezno Metropolis in the year 1000, during the momentous Gniezno Congress, when Boleslaus the Brave met the Emperor Otto III at the tomb of St. Adalbert. Then, with the consent of Pope Silvester II, the Gniezno Metropolitan See, with the bishoprics of Cracow, Kołobrzeg and Wrocław, was set up. This very important political event was noted in all the written sources of the times. The first bishop of Cracow under the archbishop of Gniezno was Poppon. We know practically nothing of his origin. The fact that Cracow was confirmed as a bishopric at this date was an honour shared by few European cities. Soon afterwards a bishop's cathedral was erected, founded by Boleslaus the Brave (d. 1025), which finally confirmed the city's Christian character.

Shortly after the death of King Boleslaus the Brave, there was unrest in Poland, mainly for social and religious reasons. To make things worse, Prince Bretislav of Bohemia took advantage of the unrest to invade the country. During his war expedition he plundered and destroyed the cathedral in Gniezno. We do not know if it was the year 1039 — as some researchers think — when Bretislav's forces entered Cracow. But we do know that it was in 1039 that Casimir the Restorer, the grandson of Boleslaus the Brave, returned to Poland from abroad. He chose Cracow as his main seat. This fact raised the city to the rank of a capital city and the first in Poland. Archbishop Aaron lived there from 1046. An intellectual centre grew up quickly around the bishop's cathedral. It is certain that after the year 1000, the Cracow cathedral scriptorium wrote the first annals. They gave the most important State and Church events. It is also probable that a cathedral school, educating not only clergy but also lay pupils, above all, the sons of dukes, was established in Cracow. In 1079, Cracow witnessed the tragedy of Bishop Stanislaus, with its far-reaching consequences, who, for reasons which we do not know much about, had a conflict with the energetic Boleslaus the Bold, the successor to Casimir the Restorer. As a result of the dramatic quarrel, Stanislaus died the death of a martyr. His body was dismembered. The effect of the bishop's murder was the banishment of Boleslaus the Bold from the country. Shortly afterwards the body of Bishop Stanislaus was brought to the cathedral and buried there. It was not long before there was a cult of Stanislaus in Cracow. This led to his canonization in 1253. Boleslaus' successor as ruler of Poland was Ladislaus Herman, the brother of the banished king. Then, for a short time the seat of the duke was moved to Płock. But Cracow still remained the first intellectual centre in Poland.

The oldest inventories of the Cracow Cathedral, from the years 1101 and 1110 have been preserved there. In the second of them there is a list of the books in the Cathedral Library. There were fifty-three volumes, containing several dozen works, which were bound together into one volume. Most of them were the works of ancient writers. There were works by five Roman authors of the golden age: Ovid, Sallustius, Statius, Persius and Terence. Reading these works was a great help in mastering correct Latin. Of the early Christian writers, Boethius and Arator, and the writings of Pope Gregory I and Isidore of Seville were read. Most of them are liturgical books.

Mention is due also to the law books, which contain works that were written in the 11th century in Western Europe. They testify to the higher education of the Cracow clergy.

In Cracow, at the beginning of the 12th century, Gallus Anonymus began to write his *Chronicle*. He was the first Polish chronicler and we do not know his Christian name. The very fact that Gallus wrote his *Chronicle* in Cracow is of great significance for the history of the city. It is a testimony to the exceptionally vital creative centre that existed there, as well as the wealth of the archives kept there and the intellectual atmosphere that was conducive to the writing of outstanding works.

In the times of Prince Ladislaus Herman (d. 1102), it is thought that the second successive Cracow cathedral was erected and completed during the reign of his son Boleslaus Wrymouth (d. 1138). Just before he died, Boleslaus Wrymouth divided the Polish State among his sons, making the eldest one the senior prince. He received a separate senior district, with Cracow as its capital, and the younger sons were subordinated to him. The will of Boleslaus Wrymouth finally established the position of Cracow in relation to the other Polish towns. From that time on it was the seat of the senior duke and the coronation insignia of Boleslaus the Bold were kept in the treasury of the cathedral. The division of Poland into duchies, the adverse side of which were the endless battles between the dukes for the Cracow throne, lasted until the 14th century. A longer period of peace was only noted during the reigns of Boleslaus the Curly (1146—73) and Casimir the Just (1173—94). The reign of Casimir the Just witnessed a particular flourishing of culture. This was the period when Master Vincent, called Kadłubek, was active at the court of the prince. He was quite an exceptional personality in Polish culture. Educated in western Europe, he was an eminent scholar, later becoming a bishop of Cracow (1208— 18) and finally, towards the end of his life he went to live in the Cistercian Abbey at Jędrzejów. Encouraged by Prince Casimir the Just, he wrote a chronicle. In its pages one can find the oldest history of Poland, Kadłubek's vision of the heroic past of the nation, full of struggles and victorious battles. Cracow played an important part in his work. Kadłubek was the first to bring the legendary Krak and his successors into Polish history. In his opinion, it was not only the fact that Cracow was the capital, but also the fact that it was the place where the relics of St. Stanislaus were kept that raised its rank. Kadłubek elevated the figure of Bishop Stanislaus to the pedestal of holiness, radiant in an aureole of miracles.

The list of volumes kept in the library in the 12th and 13th centuries was made in Kadłubek's lifetime. It contains 41 titles, the majority of which were theological writings and books on canon law. The absence of liturgical codes and ancient literature, so richly represented in the list made in 1110, is striking. The library was an example of a scholastic collection of volumes. It is probable that it belonged to Iwo Odrowąż, Kadłubek's successor at the bishopric of Cracow.

The second quarter of the 13th century was a period of violent political upheavals that followed the tragic death of Leszek the White, who was murdered in 1227. These were times of a sharp struggle for the Cracow throne between the princes Henry the Bearded and Conrad of Masovia. The turning point came in these struggles when the Tartars invaded Poland in the year 1241. An anonymous chronicler who lived in these troubled times made the following note in the *Annals of the Cracow Chapter:* "The Tartars burst into Cracow and started burning the churches, killing people regardless of their age or sex, and carrying away a great amount of loot."

The 15th century historian Jan Długosz added to this account the extra information that only Wawel and St. Andrew's Church were able to defend themselves against this oppression. All the rest of the city was destroyed and burnt. But the town quickly began to develop again after the Tartar invasion and several years later all the losses were made good. As early as 1254, Cracow was celebrating the canonization of St. Stanislaus. As a result of the endeavours of the Polish clergy, Pope Innocent IV canonized Bishop Stanislaus of Szczepanów, who died the death of a martyr. The ruling prince, Boleslaus the Bashful, as the host of this ceremony, entertained all the Polish princes who came to visit the tomb of St. Stanislaus on this occasion. But let Jan Długosz speak:

"When the emissaries of the Cracow Church, that is, Master Jakub, Dean of Skarzeszów, and Gostwin, Canon of Cracow, as well as the order of the preaching friars, and friars minor, returned from the Roman Curia, bringing with them St. Stanislaus' Canonization Bull, and were about to enter the city, all the Cracovians went out into the streets to meet them, and Prandota, the Bishop of Cracow, with all his clergy, received them by arranging a ceremonious procession of all the Cracow churches... The raising of the body of St. Stanislaus was to be on the eighth of May, which was the day the Pope in Rome had decreed that his Day should be celebrated. The Bishop of Cracow, Prandota, asked all the churches in Poland to proclaim this and tell their congregations what they should do. And when the day came, such a great multitude of people of both sexes came from all parts of Poland, and even from Hungary, to Cracow, that the city — big as it was — could not find a place for all of them and they had to camp, like sheep in the fields. Also gathered in the city for the ceremony of raising the body of the saint from the tomb, were a great number of Polish bishops, to mention only Fulko, Archbishop of Gniezno, Opizo, Abbot of Meissen, apostolic nuncio, Prandota, Bishop of Cracow Tomasz of Wrocław and Wit of Lithuania, just as great was the number of abbots, parish priests, canons and other prelates, and also the parish priests and all the clergy of Cracow and Cracow Diocese churches, who gathered to witness the event... Polish princes came to Cracow too, for instance, Boleslaus the Bashful, Prince of Cracow and Sandomierz, who was already then regarded as the Polish monarch, Przemysław, Prince of Great Poland and Poznań, Casimir, Prince of Kujawy and Łęczyca, Siemowit, Prince of Masovia, and Ladislaus, Prince of Opole. In the presence of these princes and innumerable crowds od people, the body of St. Stanislaus was taken out of the tomb, situated by the south gate of the church, by the bishops, who had gathered there for this purpose; they then washed and raised the body, and the people were glad and cried out for help from St. Stanislaus, who had been shown to them."

There was a political movement connected with the cult of the Bishop of Cracow, which in the second half of the 13th century aimed at reuniting the scattered duchies of the Polish State. It was concentrated around the saint's tomb and the Wawel Cathedral, where the coronation insignia were kept. It was believed, according to the words in the *Life of St. Stanislaus*, that as his body, which, hacked into pieces, had so miraculously grown together again, Poland too, divided into duchies, would grow together again. So it was in Cracow that the idea was born of rebuilding the Polish Kingdom.

ROMANESQUE BUILDING

Early Mediaeval Cracow was built on the left bank of the River Vistula around the fortified Wawel Castle. It consisted of several settlements on marshy land. As they developed, these settlements joined together to form larger communities, concentrated quite naturally around the routes of communication. At the beginning of the 11th century, communities of this kind grew up round Skałka (the Cliff) and to the north of Wawel Hill, on territory that was then known as Okół, and finally over the area of today's Market Place and on Salwator Hill, to mention the most important ones. Over this area, then about 50 hectares, from the second half of the 10th century, imposing buildings began to be erected, mainly sacral ones.

The biggest concentration of early Piast architecture is on Wawel Hill. The first of these buildings is the small, stone rotunda of the Blessed Virgin Mary, now known under the later name of SS. Felix and Adauctus. It is surely the oldest ducal palace chapel built on a circular ground plan, with four apses and an additional semi-circular tower, which contained a staircase. Scholars accept that this rotunda was built in the second half of the 10th century. An analogous building is the church of St. Vitus in Hradcany in Prague. Owing to the Polish-Bohemian contacts of those times, this is not without significance. The courtly character of the Rotunda of the Blessed Virgin Mary is confirmed by the recent discovery of what is thought to be a palatium by the rotunda, though many scholars see it as a mausoleum. In the direct vicinity, a piece of jewellery of gold and rock crystal has been dug up, which once decorated a diadem from about the year 1000, that is, during the reign of Boleslaus the Brave. The rotunda is one of the many churches of this type built in Poland from the 10th till the 13th centuries. Not far from the rotunda, there is a small square building; we do not know the purpose it was built for. In 1966, about 50 metres from the buildings described, the foundations of quite a large church were discovered, built on a circular ground plan with four apses. The time when this mysterious building was erected is thought to be the second half of the 10th century, and it is not out of the question that it was quite an important church, which is indicated by the tomb of an unknown dignitary discovered there.

The archaeological work on Wawel Hill is still going on, so it is very probable that it still has some secrets to yield, which means that the Romanesque buildings on Wawel Hill remain an open question. The new discoveries — including sacral buildings — that are being made, confirm the hypothesis of the importance of Wawel Hill in the times of the first Piasts.

An important event in the history of Cracow was the formal recognition of the bishopric (1000) and in consequence of this fact, the building of a cathedral for the Bishop. The small interior of the palace chapel was no longer enough. It was most probably towards the end of the reign of Boleslaus the Brave that the building of the first cathedral was started. Fragments of this building have remained under the west wing of the present royal palace. The building was started after the signing of the peace of Bautzen (Budziszyn; 1018), which ended the many years of fighting between Boleslaus the Brave and the Emperor Henry II. From the fragments that have survived, one can draw the conclusion that it must have been a monumental church. In accordance with mediaeval custom, the main altar faced East and the church had one nave and two aisles and a transept. Under the presbytery, there was a crypt supported by eight columns. Carved ornamentation has survived (a column, a slab which is ornamented with a plaited pattern) — a testimony to the level of the interior decoration, which is attributed to craftsmen from distant Italy. Attention has been drawn to the architectural analogy between St. Michael's Church in Hildesheim, the Cathedral in Merseburg and Cracow Cathedral. These artistic links with the Saxon environment are fully justified by the lively political contacts and dynastic links of the first Piasts, Mieszko I and Boleslaus the Brave. There were plenty of occasions for them to see the culture and buoyant artistic life of the Saxons and transfer their newest architectural designs onto their own ground. It is generally thought that the building of the cathedral was never completed. The building may have been stopped when Boleslaus the Brave died suddenly after his coronation in Gniezno in 1025. The first Wawel Cathedral had St. Wenceslas, the Bohemian duke, as its patron. His cult in Bohemia at the close of the 10th century was very lively, and King Boleslaus the Brave, who was a relation of the saint through his mother Dobrava, made Wenceslas the patron saint of the Cracow Cathedral. The building, erected with such difficulty, was destroyed by an unknown cataclysm and all that survived was the eastern part, which, in the first half of the 11th century, was made into the Church of St. Gereon. In the late 11th century, people began to think about building a new cathedral. During the reign of Boleslaus the Bold (1058—79), the Polish church organization was restored and the final decision was taken to make Gniezno its metropolis. Some researchers attribute the foundation of the new Cracow Cathedral to Boleslaus the Bold, although tradition and some other scholars attribute it to Ladislaus Herman (1079—1102), calling it the "Herman" Cathedral.

The last twenty years of the 11th century in the history of Cracow were rather mysterious. The above-mentioned conflict (of which we do not know the details) between King Boleslaus the Bold and the Bishop of Cracow, Stanislaus, led to the martyr's death of the bishop, while the king was banished from the country. The chronicler known as Gallus Anonymus wrote: "How it happened that King Boleslaus was banished from Poland would be to tell a very long story; but one thing can be said, that being an anointed man he should not have punished another anointed man for any sin by a bodily punishment. For it did him a lot of harm to punish a sin by committing another sin and for betrayal decreed that the Bishop's arms and legs be cut off." The successor to Boleslaus was his younger brother, Prince Ladislaus Herman. It is thought that the cathedral was destroyed by fire during his reign and he came forward with the initiative to build another church. It was situated near the site of the first cathedral, a little to the west of it. The western part of the cathedral was completed at the end of the century and, before 1118, the crypt of St. Leonard was finished. According to the chronicle of Jan Długosz, the cathedral was completed by Herman's son, Prince Boleslaus Wrymouth. On 20 April 1142, Bishop Robert ceremoniously consecrated the new building. It was built of limestone, extracted from the nearby quarry at Krzemionki. The cathedral was of the basilica type, with two towers on the west side. The tower of the Silver Bells and the crypt of St. Leonard have survived to this day, giving the best idea of the architecture of the "Herman" cathedral. The noble proportions of the crypt, the care that was taken with form and excellent workmanship, all testify to the high artistic standards of the whole building. The second cathedral was also furnished with essential, suitable liturgical equipment. In the oldest cathedral inventories, 32 apart from books, the liturgical robes and vessels were also mentioned. The cathedral had over 300 of them, which for those times was a huge number. They included gold chalices, crosses, candlesticks and very valuable reliquaries, and also chasubles, copes and cloths. These things, mentioned in both inventories, glorified God's praise, and these magnificent paraments could be seen in all their glory when a long ceremony was celebrated in the cathedral. The Cathedral Treasury also kept the royal crown of Boleslaus the Bold and the spear of St. Maurice, a symbol of sovereign power, which was offered to Boleslaus the Brave by the Emperor Otto III. Not many of the furnishings of the cathedral have survived to this day. There is a 13th century Sicilian-made coffer. The pride of the cathedral collection is the 15th century cross made from two 13th century ducal diadems, belonging the Boleslaus the Bashful and his wife Kinga. They were decorated with hunting scenes and pictures of knights fighting, and scholars think that this priceless historic relic was made in a Venetian or Hungarian workshop. St. Stanislaus' mitre, made of expensive materials, ornamented with pearls and precious stones, comes from the same period as the ducal diadems referred to above. It is one of the most valuable embroidered articles in Europe and is thought to have been worn at the ceremony of the canonization of St. Stanislaus (1254). The other items mentioned in the inventory have been lost, but those that have survived the storms of our history are ample proof of how the "Herman" cathedral was equipped. Valuable folios ornamented with miniatures were brought from abroad, for instance the early 12th century Book of the Evangelists of the St. Emmeram Monastery from Regensburg, which contains, among other things, likenesses of the abbots, evangelists, and of the Emperor Henry V. No traces of the Romanesque polychromes have survived in the Wawel Cathedral, though the historic buildings that have survived on Polish territory lead one to assume that it was ornamented with them. The Romanesque cathedral survived till the early 14th century.

Beside the cathedral two other large churches were built in the 11th century, St. Michael's and St. George's and to the east of Boleslaus the Brave's cathedral, on a piece of higher ground, a ducal castle, the seat of the Polish ruler was built. All the other buildings on the hill were built of timber.

In this period too, the first stone buildings went up around Wawel Hill. The magnificent Church of St. Andrew, with its two towers on the western façade, began to be built at the end of the 11th century at the foot of Wawel Hill. It was founded by a state dignitary during the reign of Ladislaus Herman, the all-powerful palatine Sieciech. This monumental Romanesque church — the second largest after the cathedral — has lasted till our days. The nearby Church of St. Martin was built probably in the 12th century and a little later — probably at the beginning of the 13th century — the Church of St. Mary Magdalene. All these churches were in the strongly fortified settlement known as Okół where there was the main trading and handicraft centre of early mediaeval Cracow. Apart from Wawel, this was the oldest settlement. The main trade routes went through it as did the road leading to Wawel Hill.

On the other hand, in the area of today's Market Place, there was already a little church in the 10th century (which was reconstructed in the early 12th century), and today it is known as St. Adalbert's. Other Romanesques churches — that of St. John, St. Nicholas and the collegiate church of St. Florian, as well as the churches of the Most Holy Saviour (the end of the 10th century) built near the city of those days, and of St. Benedict (The latter was combined with an oblong palatium building; the purpose for which it was built is not known.) are only known today from the foundations that have survived and Romanesque remains in the walls of existing buildings.

Before the granting of the *locatio civitatis* to the city in the middle of the 13th century, there were nearly 30 churches in Cracow, an exceptionally high number in contemporary Europe. According to the description of the Arab geographer al Idrisi in the 12th century, it was a beautiful, large city with dense buildings and numerous population, market places, vineyards, gardens and was full of learned men. From the 10th to the 13th centuries, Cracow was a large mediaeval city and one of the few metropolises of contemporary Europe.

With the passing of time, the Okół settlement developed from a strongly fortified defence unit into an open settlement with a population of merchants and artisans, and the city began to spread towards the north. As early as the 12th century the Church of the Holy Trinity, described in written sources as the parish church of Cracow (which was handed over to the Dominicans in 1222), stood in what we know today as Dominican Square. Soon after, opposite the Dominican Monastery, the Franciscans settled there, too (1237), as the second of the fashionable mendicant orders of those times.

Before the middle of the 13th century, the following churches were built: St. Mary's and the Holy Cross Church with a hospital (run by the Holy Ghost Fathers). According to estimates, the city then had a population of 2,000. This was the time when the municipal community administration began to develop (the name of the *scultetus* Piotr can be found in written sources from the years 1228 and 1230 and of the *scultetus* Salomon in 1250). Ever more frequently researchers are coming out in favour of the hypothesis that in the first quarter of the 13th century, Cracow was granted some kind of location privilege by Prince Leszek the White. The central district of the city was to be Okół, with the largest number of churches (after Wawel Hill) and a Market Place round the Church of St. Mary Magdalene. The first location of Cracow in Okół can be treated as an introduction to a bigger undertaking, namely, the so-called Great Location in 1257, organizing the city by the Magdeburg Law, following the example of Silesian towns. All this happened barely a dozen or so years after the terrible invasion of the Tartars (1241), which only succeeded in checking the development of Cracow for a short time.

CHAPTER II · THE MEDIAEVAL SHAPE OF THE CITY

THE *LOCATIO CIVITATIS* OF CRACOW BY GERMAN LAW

Visitors to Cracow are amazed at the unusual town planning impetus of the old city, seen mainly in the huge Market Place, covering an area of four hectares and fulfilling its function superbly to this very day. In addition, the chequered pattern of the streets and the logical planning of the city within the former fortifications (today the Planty Gardens) are further proofs of the good development of the city in the Middle Ages. The year 1257 was a turning point in this respect in the history of Cracow. On 5 June, Duke Boleslaus the Bashful, his wife Kinga and his mother Grzymisława granted the *locatio civitatis* which gave the city rights on the lines of the Magdeburg charter. It was an act establishing legal and economic relations, marking out the boundaries of the city and therefore the planning of the areas destined for settlement. The city gained complete autonomy, became an independent legal unit with its own social system and courts of law. Its administrator became the vassal of the ruler and represented the prince in the city. With the passing of time, a municipal council was formed, which gradually became independent of the ruler.

The provisions of the *locatio civitatis* were introduced successively over a period of time. But the Market Place was marked out at once and so were the plots where houses were to be built. In the location area of the city, the existing churches were included, which caused some asymmetry in the plan of Cracow.

The plan of the city is, in principle, a square with rounded corners, concentrated round the Market Place, which measures 200 m × 200 m. From each side of the Market Place there are three streets leading out at right angles, to be crossed halfway down by transverse streets. In the southern part of the city this regularity is missing, which is explained by the buildings erected before the *locatio civitatis* was granted. Cracow is divided into sectors by streets, these sectors in turn being divided into equal plots for residential building. The markets were held in the Market Place, where buildings were quickly erected for trading: Sukiennice (Cloth Hall), shops, scales, etc. It was here that the life of the city was concentrated. An auxiliary Market Place was situated in the eastern part of the city, the so-called Small Market Place. Outside the boundaries of Cracow the economic base supplying the city sprang up: mills, breweries, sawmills, slaughter houses, brickyards and potteries.

Shortly after the next Tartar invasion (1259—60), which devastated Little Poland, the development of the city continued with impetus. The area of Cracow had by then reached a little more than 30 hectares. The city, which was roughly in the shape of a square, included monumental buildings on the south-east edge, those that were built before the *locatio civitatis* was granted. All the Romanesque buildings in this area were absorbed into the city. Okół and the settlements surrounding the Church of St. Florian, the Church on the Sand (Na Piasku), and the Churches of St. Nicholas, St. Lawrence, St. James and the Church on the Cliff (Na Skałce) were all outside the boundaries of contemporary Cracow. Work was continued on the realization of both earlier and new plans too. The Dominican monks gradually built their church. Boleslaus the Bashful founded a church for the Franciscan monks and the Church of St. Mark, both of which were completed in the second half of the 13th century. These brick buildings had features that were definitely Gothic. The church of the Franciscan monks (c. 1269) was built on a ground plan like a Greek cross, with a rectangular closing of the presbytery. The church built by the Dominican monks (c. 1250) has the same kind of presbytery and in the first half of the 15th century was converted from a hall-like building into a two-aisle basilica. Also, the Franciscan church was made longer in a westerly direction in the first half of the 15th century.

Together with the erection of sacral buildings, residential building proceeded, especially round the magnificent Market Place. At the turn of the 13th and 14th centuries, a new parish church of the Blessed Virgin Mary was built on the site of an earlier parish church. It was a hall-like church with a nave and two aisles. Remains of that church can be seen in the walls of the present church. The Cloth Hall (stalls selling cloth) and the Town Hall, provided for in the location act, were built at the same time. The problem of the earliest fortifications after the *locatio civitatis* is still an open question. It can be assumed that, shortly after 1257, fortifications made of timber, stone and earth were built. It is significant that the location act does not mention fortifications. Most probably, after the second Tartar invasion (1259—60), people began to think more about the defence of the city and began work on linking up the overflow arms to the river and the marshes surrounding Cracow by a tributary of the River Rudawa (Młynówek), which in future was to supply the moats of the city with water. But the earliest mention of the fortifications of Cracow is as late as the last quarter of the 13th century. During the reign of Leszek the Black, in 1285, there was a battle against Conrad, Prince of Czersk. The burghers of Cracow defended the city from this attack, remaining true to the vow of fealty they had made to Leszek the Black and as a reward received the privilege to fortify Cracow. This was what decided the future territorial development of the city, initiating work on the fortification system, which marked out the boundaries of mediaeval Cracow. This was another fact of significance for Cracow, for it ensured the defensibility of the city and the safety of its inhabitants. It also increased the strength of Cracow. During the third Tartar invasion (1287) the city was able to defend itself, thanks partly to the fortifications already built.

The first mention of the oldest city gate is from the year 1289; the defence of the gate was entrusted to the Butchers' Guild. The main intensification of the building of fortifications came during the fifteen years' reign of Wenceslas II, King of Bohemia and Poland; information about the Bohemians' intensive work on fortifying Cracow in the years 1291—1305 is given in written sources. At the turn of the 13th and 14th centuries, Cracow, then consisting of two independent municipal organisms, was surrounded by a wall with gates which guarded the inlet-outlet trade routes which existed before the granting of the *locatio civitatis*.

THE CAPITAL OF THE POLISH STATE

The turn of the 13th and 14th centuries was a period of intensified struggle for the unification of the Polish state. After the unexpected death of Przemysł II (1296), the Prince of Great Poland, who ruled the Cracow region for some time, claims to the Polish throne were put forward by the son-in-law of the dead Prince, the Bohemian King Wenceslas II and by the Prince of Kujawy, Ladislaus the Short, the brother of Leszek the Black. Finally, in 1300 Wenceslas was crowned King of Poland, which opened the way for Bohemian influences in Poland. The anti-Bohemian opposition was headed by Ladislaus the Short, who was backed by the knighthood and promises of aid from Hungarian noblemen. He also made continuous diplomatic endeavours in the international forum, mainly at the Papal Curia. As early as 1304, Ladislaus made an attempt to free Poland from the rule of Wenceslas II. The situation was made easier by the death of Wenceslas II (1305) and shortly afterwards the treacherous murder of his son Wenceslas III (1306). Ladislaus mastered Cracow and Sandomierz and from the very beginning made Cracow the centre of the state he was rebuilding. He was very generous in distributing privileges among the burghers of Cracow, who had strong economic links with the Kingdom of Bohemia and were therefore rather reluctant to accept the Polish prince. Wishing to win over the inhabitants of Cracow, he conferred important rights upon them (the right to buy and store; 1306). From that time, in accordance with the provisions of these rights, all the merchants who came to Cracow had to exhibit their goods for sale and could only take them out of the city if nobody wanted to buy them. The most important raw material carried in transit — Hungarian copper — could therefore only be purchased by Cracovian merchants, who, in turn, sold it in western Europe, mainly in the cities of wealthy Flanders. These rights were the basis of the wealth of the Cracow burghers.

36

However, the first years of the reign of Ladislaus the Short were rather turbulent. It was not long before the German patriciate revolted (1311). They were headed in the revolt against the prince by the magistrate of Cracow, Albert, who was the representative of the party of the Bohemian King, John of Luxembourg. Ladislaus the Short was not long in suppressing this revolt (1312), reorganizing the municipal authorities and making them dependent on him and limiting the privileges and autonomy of the city. The hereditary post of magistrate was annulled. A ban on the use of the German language in the municipal records was also issued. All documents began to be written in Latin. Those responsible for the revolt were punished severely. A contemporary chronicler wrote as follows: "Duke Ladislaus, on entering... the town again, imprisoned some of the burghers and put a strong guard on them. Then he ordered them to be pulled through the whole city tied to horses and then pulled outside the city to the gallows, where they were hung ignominously and then the Duke decreed that they should be left hanging there till their tendons rotted and till the muscles holding their bones together loosened." Ladislaus the Short then founded a New City in Okół (*Nova Civitas in Okol*), to balance the over-Germanized Cracow.

When he took Great Poland, this made Ladislaus the ruler of the most politically important lands of Poland. The process of uniting the country came to an end with the coronation of Ladislaus the Short and his queen Jadwiga (Hedwig). On 20 January 1320, the Archbishop of Gniezno, Janisław, crowned the royal pair in the old Romanesque Cracow Cathedral. This was indeed a truly historic event. The chronicler Jan Długosz thus described that noble ceremony:

"When at last Sunday came, on the name day of St. Fabian and St. Sebastian, people of all ranks and stations, prelates and Polish noblemen, went to Cracow. During the high Mass of the Holy Spirit, the Archbishop of Gniezno, Janisław, assisted by the Bishop of Cracow, Muskata, the Bishop of Poznań, Domarat, and abbots from Tyniec, Mogilno, Jędrzejów and Brzesk, in copes and mitres, and a great crowd of wealthy lords and gentry, anointed Duke Ladislaus the Short as King and his wife Jadwiga, the daughter of the Prince of Poznań, Boleslaus, as Queen. He then crowned them with royal crowns, which, with the orb, sceptre and other royal insignia were also transferred from Gniezno to Cracow. This was an extremely solemn day, but a day of general joy... And from that time onwards the Cracow Cathedral received for the first time the distinguished privilege of being the place where the coronations of Polish kings took place and would always take place... It was also decided to hold the coronation ceremonies of Polish kings and queens in the Cracow Cathedral in the future...".

The coronation of Ladislaus the Short was an act which finally decided that Cracow would be the capital of the Poland resurrected from the division into duchies. The fact that the royal court was in Cracow, the court ceremonies this involved, and the meetings of monarchs held there had an animating effect on the city; its population increased and so did its wealth.

After a stormy reign, thirteen years after his coronation, King Ladislaus the Short died at the castle in Cracow. He was buried in the Cracow Cathedral and from then on it fulfilled the function of the Polish royal necropolis. Ladislaus' successors, their spouses and members of the reigning family were all laid to rest in the vaults of the Cathedral.

Ladislaus' son, King Casimir the Great (1333—70) had a difficult task in consolidating the political existence of the Polish Kingdom, normalizing relations with neighbouring countries, and finally making the former duchies into one whole, as well as promoting the economic and cultural development of the country. Casimir the Great concentrated all this work in the capital of the state — Cracow. In carrying out his political plans, Casimir was assisted by the knights of the Cracow region and by Cracow burghers.

As regards general state matters the proximity of Bohemia was very important to Cracow. By means of feudal vassalage (1327, 1329) the duchies of Silesia came under the rule of John of Luxembourg and became part of Bohemia. Finally, in 1339, Casimir the Great gave up his rights to the Silesian duchies, whose rulers recognized the right of John of Luxembourg to rule them. By this, the Bohemian frontier was moved nearer to Cracow, constituting a serious threat to the city. This already became evident in 1345, when in a short war with the Bohemians over Silesia, John of Luxembourg's troops came right up to the walls of Cracow and laid siege to the city that was faithful to Casimir the Great. Cracow, surrounded by walls, was not an easy city to take. In order to ensure that in the future the capital city would not be endangered, the king quickly built a number of fortified castles on the Polish-Bohemian border. They were at Ojców, Będzin, Olkusz, Olsztyn, Lelów, Krzepice, and, near Cracow, Lanckorona and Skawina.

At the same time, the king ordered that two independent towns should be built outside Cracow: Kazimierz situated to the south of Wawel Hill, and Kleparz situated to the north of the city surrounding the collegiate Church of St. Florian. These were "satellite" towns in relation to the capital city. Only Kazimierz was fortified. Kleparz never had defence walls. Kazimierz was divided from Cracow by the Stradom settlement, subordinate to it, and was surrounded by the River Vistula on all sides, and so possessed natural defence conditions. To the west of Cracow, Garbary, a settlement of artisans, was organized, which had full autonomy and a local administration council and administrator's office. So it was during the reign of Casimir the Great that Cracow took shape with its surrounding "satellites": the towns of Kazimierz (1335), Kleparz (1366) and Garbary. This form remained as it was, with only slight changes, until the beginning of the 20th century.

The city received from Casimir the Great a confirmation of the privileges it already had and some new trading privileges, conducive to economic development. The king took care to ensure that Polish towns got the lion's share of transit trade. This policy was facilitated by the conclusion of a peace treaty with the Order of the Teutonic Knights in Kalisz (1343) and the taking of Halicz Rus, that was economically linked with Little Poland, by the monarch. The main role in this policy went to Cracow.

Also Casimir the Great called into being a higher court of German Law at the Royal Castle (1356) the aim of which was to issue decisions on disputes between the king's towns, instead of sending the matter to Magdeburg, as had been the practice so far. The year 1358 marks the issue by the monarch of what has been called the Great Privilege, which confirmed the rights already possessed by Cracow, increasing the municipal income and giving the city important rights by setting up a court of justice for people living in the suburbs.

As the capital of the Kingdom of Poland, Cracow lived through a period of splendour and political and economic importance during the reign of Casimir the Great. Its situation at the place where the trade routes (established at the turn of the 13th and 14th centuries) crossed: south-north (going through Košice—Nowy Sącz—Bochnia—Cracow—Piotrków—Toruń—Gdańsk), and east-west (going from the Black Sea Coast—Lvov—Przemyśl—Jarosław—Tarnów—Bochnia—Cracow—Wrocław — through to further towns in the west) did much to help Cracow gain considerable possibilities of economic development and therefore the accumulation of wealth by its inhabitants. Apart from the patriciate, mainly of German origin, numerous other foreigners also came to Cracow, including Italian merchants. Artisans' guilds were organized and artisans had seats in the municipal council.

The fame of the capital of Poland spread all over Europe. It was the place where the king organized a congress of European monarchs, which was held in September 1364. It was attended by distinguished guests invited by Casimir the Great: Louis, King of Hungary, Charles IV, King of Bohemia and the Emperor; Waldemar, King of Denmark, Peter, King of Cyprus, as well as Otto, Margrave of Brandenburg, Ziemowit, Prince of Masovia and several Silesian princes. The debates concerned the setting up of an anti-Turkish league. The Cracow congress allowed Casimir to demonstrate his political power and the prosperity of his country. An example of the wealth of the Cracow burghers was the municipal councillor, Mikołaj Wierzynek, who, with the king's permission, entertained at his home on behalf of the whole city, all the royal guests of the king. The feast at Wierzynek's home is now a legend. This is what Długosz wrote about it:

"The Cracow councillor, Wierzynek, the Steward of the Royal Estate, as mentioned above, decided that he too should entertain. He invited five kings and all the princes and guests to a banquet at his home. When he received permission from the monarchs to seat his guests according to his own discretion — he gave the first and most magnificent place to the Polish King Casimir the Great, the second place to Charles, King of Rome and Bohemia, the third place to the King of Hungary, the fourth to the King of Cyprus and the last place to the King of Denmark... He served very elaborate dishes and in addition he offered magnificent gifts to all his guests during the banquet. But the gift that he presented to the Polish King Casimir, in front of all the other kings, was so very lavish, costing more than a hundred thousand florins, it aroused not only admiration but surprise, too."

There is no doubt that the greatest cultural undertaking of those times was the opening of a university in Cracow. There had been a cathedral school in Cracow since the 11th century and, at least from the second quarter of the 13th century, there had been a parish school by St. Mary's Church. But to get a higher education one had to go abroad and the high costs of travel and education closed the door to a degree to those who did not have enough money to cover these expenses. There was a growing demand for educated people with the development of the monarchy, so the king applied to the Papal Curia for permission to open a university in Cracow in 1354; the result was the opening in 1364, by virtue of a special Papal and Royal Privilege, of a "studium generale" — the first higher school in Poland. It is worth adding that the Cracow University was the second university, after the one in Prague (1348), to be set up in Central Europe, earlier than any of the German universities. In the foundation document issued by the king, we read: "We have decided to select, decide upon and furnish a place in our city of Cracow, where a general school will flourish in every department, and in the future we would like this document to ensure its existence for ever. So let it be powerful, the finest example of learning we have, giving us men of great maturity, who will give us excellent council, examples of all the virtues, men very learned in various skills; let a refreshing spring spout up, and from its riches let every man who wishes to learn something drink his fill. To Cracow let all those come freely and safely, not only the inhabitants of our Kingdom and neighbouring lands, but also others from various parts of the world, who desire to win the famous pearl of knowledge."

The organization of the new university was based on models taken from the universities at Bologna and Padua, and the most significant was the law department, needed so badly by the Polish state. The founding of the university was, without exaggeration, the greatest historical merit of Casimir the Great, although during his reign that last of the Piast rulers showed that he could also be an eminent statesman, strategist, manager, and, above all a monarch of inventiveness, a man who cared for the development of the culture of his country. A chronicler of his times, Janko of Czarnków, evaluated the building activities of the king as follows:

"This King was over all other monarchs of Poland in governing the country; for, like a second Solomon, he raised his work to the level of greatness — he built walls round the city, castles, houses... All the towns and castles had very strong walls and high towers, surrounded by exceptionally deep moats and other defence installations, as an embellishment of the people, for the protection and care of the Polish Kingdom."

After the death of Casimir the Great the throne went to his nephew, the Hungarian King Louis (1370—82) of the Angevin dynasty. This marked the beginning of a turbulent period in the history of Poland, full of internal disturbances and struggles between parties. As he did not have a son, Louis issued the Košice Privilege (1374), whereby he named one of his daughters as his successor to the throne of Poland. After his death (1382), the Polish nobles, after a long hesitation, named young Jadwiga as successor to Louis and she was crowned queen in Cracow Cathedral in 1384. A year later, the historic Polish-Lithuanian Union was concluded at Krevo. By virtue of this agreement, the Lithuanian Grand Duke Jagiełło and his subjects adopted the Roman Catholic faith, he married Jadwiga and joined Lithuania to the Polish Kingdom. So Cracow then became the capital of a huge state of nearly a million sq. km., composed of Lithuania and Ruthenias, as well as Polish lands.

In January 1386, Jagiełło was proclaimed king of Poland, on 15 February he was christened in Cracow and three days later his wedding with Jadwiga took place. On 4 March, Jagiełło was crowned king in the Cathedral on Wawel Hill. During the reign of Ladislaus Jagiełło (1386—1434), a decisive battle was fought by the Polish and Lithuanian knights against the Teutonic Knights at Grunwald (1410). Jagiełło hung several dozen banners, won in this victorious battle, by the tomb of St. Stanislaus in the Wawel Cathedral. Cracow celebrated the triumph of the Polish and Lithuanian forces splendidly. The celebration was thus described by Jan Długosz:

"... On the day of St. Catherine, surrounded by a numerous group of prelates and knights carrying before him the unfurled banners of the Teutonic Knights, won in the great Battle of Grunwald, he came first to the town of Kazimierz and from there went to Skałka. Here, after having made his devotions to the holy relics kept there, he went on to the Cracow Castle and to the Cathedral, preceded by the banners of the Teutonic Knights, and in the church named after St. Stanislaus in Cracow, put all the banners there, in memory of the famous victory; they hang on the walls there to this very day, on the right and left sides, to show his own people and foreigners a great spectacle, the triumph of the King and the defeat of the Teutonic Knights...".

The period of Jagiełło's reign also saw the revival of Cracow University which suspended its activity shortly after the death of Casimir the Great. At the end of the 14th century, Queen Jadwiga and Jagiełło applied to the Papal Curia for permission to re-open the university, together with the right to set up a theological department. The university, according to the royal conception, was to educate the people living on the huge territories of Poland, Lithuania and Ruthenia, and contribute to the Christianization of the lands gained. The queen gave all her valuables and jewellery to the University in her will. King Ladislaus Jagiełło, Bishop Piotr Wysz and a professor at the Prague University, Mateusz of Cracow, also contributed to the foundation fund. On 26 July, in the year 1400, Ladislaus Jagiełło issued a foundation privilege for the university. The Cracow "Studium" gradually came to life again. The houses purchased with Queen Jadwiga's gift were used as lecture rooms and the offices of the university. Not long after this, the first students' hostels were opened. The organization of the university was changed in relation to 1364. This time it was modelled on the French Sorbonne, not on Italian universities. Whereas Casimir the Great had laid stress on the development of the law department, now, in connection with the christianization of Lithuania, the stress was put on theology. The Bishop of Cracow became the chancellor of the university and approved all degrees. Stanisław of Skalbmierz, a scholar of European fame, was elected the first rector of the university.

It was not long before the university won international fame. It should be mentioned, at this point, that in the period of the Great Schism (in the first half of the 15th century) the authority of the centres of learning represented by the universities was considerably strengthened. In the Church, a heated dispute broke out about the superiority of the ecumenical council over the pope and the idea of conciliarism was the subject of lively discussions at ecumenical councils. At the Council of Constance (1414) the Cracow University and the king were represented by the Rector, Paweł Włodkowic. In a well prepared treatise, he was decidedly in favour of the idea of conciliarism, at the same time criticizing the exploitation of the country by the papacy. He also defended the right of non-Christian countries to self-determination, which was a new doctrine. The Cracow University also took part in later ecumenical councils.

The Law Department of the Cracow University achieved very high standards. And apart from that there were other departments that were developing particularly well, namely: Astrology, Mathematics, Astronomy and Theology. Among the outstanding professors, mention is due to Jan Dąbrówka, the astrologer Marcin of Żurawica, the astronomer Marcin Bylica of Olkusz, the mathematician and astronomer Wojciech of Brudzewo. Nicolaus Copernicus of Toruń was a student of the Cracow University, enrolling in 1491. It is thought that it was during his several ·years' studies at Cracow (1491—95), that his heliocentric theory was born, later to be published in his epoch-making work *De revolutionibus orbium coelestium* (1543).

The University very quickly met up with the idea of humanism flowing into Poland from the South of Europe. The participation of professors in ecumenical councils, and numerous trips abroad all contributed to their having direct contact with the Italian Renaissance milieu (the intellectual movement was mainly concentrated in Medicean Florence and Papal Rome). Interest in the classical culture and the works of ancient authors began earlier in Cracow and cultural events in Italy were known there. An important role in this was played by the court of the Cracow Bishop, Zbigniew Oleśnicki, who ruled supreme during the reign of Ladislaus III (1434—44), the son of Ladislaus Jagiełło. A copy of the work of Livy was brought from the south, which was shortly to serve Jan Długosz (d. 1480) when he was writing his *History of Poland*. Długosz — it must be emphasized — was also a student at the university. The stay in Cracow of the famous Italian humanist, Filippo Buonaccorsi (Callimachus), one of the founders of the Rome Academy, who was educating the sons of King Casimir IV, made a major contribution to the promotion of humanism in Cracow and imbued the scholarly and intellectual movement with the humanist spirit. This outstanding humanist's royal pupils were before long to sit on European thrones: Ladislaus became King of Bohemia in 1471, and in 1490, the King of Hungary too; John Albert, Alexander and Sigismund reigned in turn over Poland. From 1488, the German humanist Conrad Celtis stayed for a short time in Cracow, lecturing "modus epistolandi" in one of the students' hostels. He set up the first literary society — *Sodalitas Litteraria Vistulana*. University professors were active in the society, among others, Wojciech of Brudzewo and Wawrzyniec Korwin.

To Jan Ursinus, a friend of Celtis, we owe the description of an excursion to the suburbs, to the estate of doctor Charamanus, situated just beyond the Cobblers' Gate, near the monastery of the Carmelite monks. Ursinus relates that the company, after going into the water naked, "began to shout like drunkards and bantered with each other, so that anyone watching us could have taken us for madmen... Our wives stood nearby and also maidens, some of whom were beautiful, adorned with gold and precious stones and bedecked with flowers. Although they were too ashamed to join us in our games, they looked at us and were merry and laughing at what we did... Miss Constance, standing out from the others with her beautiful figure, wanted to sting Jerzy Turzo with a nettle, but fell into the water up to her waist, which caused a lot of merriment". Further on, a walk after lunch is described, during which glasses of Hungarian and Cretan wines were handed round: "We wandered about for a long time, some of us were singing, others playing jokes or cuddling their wives or the maidens. Returning to the stream, we sat on the grass and drank sour milk to cool our heated brows. Then we watched the country people and the dancers till sunset." This pastoral picture gives what is, to some extent, the real atmosphere of the social life of the Cracow humanists at the end of the 15th century.

The lively scholastic and intellectual movement gathered round the university, radiated to the whole of Poland, and also outside its boundaries during the reign of Casimir IV (1447—92), thus confirming the role of Cracow, not only as a political capital, but also as a centre of the intellectual life of the country. And it was in Cracow that the first Polish printing house was opened, and not long after this Cracow became famous for its printing houses.

Parallel to the nascent humanist trend, religious life also flourished in the second half of the 15th century. The stay in Cracow of the preacher John of Capistrano (1453—54) led to an exceptional upsurge of religious feeling. Shortly afterwards, in the monastery of the Bernardine monks, Szymon of Lipnica became famous for his virtues and he was later beatified. Others who won fame for their saintly lives were Brother Izjasz Boner, from the Augustinian Order, Michał Giedroyć, a monk at the monastery of St. Mark, and Stanisław Kazimierczyk, a priest from the Congregation of Canons Regular of the Lateran. No less famous in his lifetime was John Cantius (d. 1473), a university professor and outstanding theologist, canonized in 1767. This remarkable upsurge of religious feeling was in close connection with the anti-Hussite activity of the Polish clergy, led by Cardinal Zbigniew Oleśnicki, which played a considerable role in inciting devotion, shallow religious feelings, and multiplying donations to the Church.

At the end of the Middle Ages, Cracow — the capital of the great state of the Jagiellons — was at the peak of its splendour. The political stabilization that followed the Peace of Toruń (1466), which ended the war with the Teutonic Knights, and the regaining of Pomerania with Gdańsk, contributed to a flourishing economic and cultural development. Peace in the country, the cultural patronage of Casimir IV and his Queen, Elizabeth of Habsburg, all led to the cultural and artistic development of Cracow. The city then had a population of nearly 10,000 and resounded with the voices of the Polish and foreign students attending the university.

In 1493, Hartmann Schedel's *Chronicon mundi* appeared in Nuremberg. It contained the oldest view of Cracow and a description of the city. It reads thus:

"Cracow is surrounded by a high double wall with towers, gates and fortifications and the River Rudawa supplies its moats with water, turning the wheels of numerous mills; there are many beautiful houses and huge churches in the city."

GOTHIC ART

The building of the third successive cathedral on Wawel Hill marked the beginning of truly Gothic architecture in Cracow. In 1305, on the day after the ceremonies marking the canonization of St. Stanislaus (8 May) the Romanesque cathedral, remembering the times of Ladislaus Herman, went up in flames. The lead roof melted, the timber ceiling beams fell down and the walls of the cathedral were scorched badly. The fire was quickly put out, but the losses were enormous. Just after the fire had been put out, work was started at once on safeguarding the building. The church was covered with a roof and new ceiling beams were put in. And so the cathedral was to remain for a dozen or so years. Probably at the beginning of 1320, the building of the new cathedral was started. Bishop Nanker and King Ladislaus the Short are regarded as the founders. The work was carried out in two basic phases. In the years 1320—46 the presbytery and its precincts, and then in the years 1349—64, the two-aisle body of the church (the main nave and the side aisles) were built. Stone was used as the building material, only in the presbytery was the stone mixed with brick. Also at this time, the majority of the chapels surrounding the aisles of the cathedral were built. At last came the day when the work of several generations was crowned. On 28 March 1364, in the presence of King Casimir the Great, the venerable Archbishop of Gniezno, Jarosław Bogoria, ceremoniously consecrated the royal cathedral. From that time, it became the main shrine of the Polish Kingdom, the place where kings were crowned and laid to rest, as well as the place where all kinds of magnificent church and state ceremonies were held. It fulfilled both liturgical and state functions.

The cathedral on Wawel Hill was a stone, two-aisle basilica with a transept and an apse surrounding the rectangular presbytery. The special construction system applied in building the cathedral, used very often in later years in the building of many Gothic churches in Cracow and Little Poland, is different from the Gothic constructions used generally in the western European churches. It consists in joining the bearing pillar to the buttress and the elimination of the flying buttresses. This system was called the Cracow or the pillar-buttress system. Also, for the first time in Poland, the singular system of vaulting with three supporting pillars was used, already known in French and English mediaeval architecture for a long time. The plan is based on two Silesian churches: the Cistercian one in Henryków and the Cathedral in Wrocław. Respect was shown during the building to the earlier fragments, which were included in the walls of the new edifice (the crypt of St. Leonard and the Tower of the Silver Bells).

From the outside, the cathedral looks quite modest in comparison with the major cathedrals of Western Europe. Its Gothic character shows immediately in the slim gable of the façade, decorated with a statue of St. Stanislaus, a rosette and a Piast eagle. At the sides, the façade is hidden behind two 15th century Jagiellon chapels, completely covered with Gothic decoration. Between the two chapels is the iron door, which witnessed the times of Casimir the Great, and is ornamented with many royal monograms, consisting of the letter "K" (in Polish the name was spelt *Kazimierz*). At the sides of the body of the cathedral the triangular gables of the transept can be seen and on the north side, by the Sigismund Tower, there is the 15th century building of the Cathedral Treasury. On the south side, the cathedral is surrounded with a wreath of chapels, built in the Renaissance and Baroque periods, which create a characteristic whole, such as will not be found outside Poland. The constructional and spatial elements that crystallized in the cathedral on Wawel Hill were later imitiated in other churches in Cracow and elsewhere in Poland.

The Cracow cathedral was, above all, the main church of the diocese, the seat of the bishop and also the church used for court ceremonies. But the most important for the town was St. Mary's Church, "the burghers' cathedral". It was built in the Market Place, on the site of another building dating from the period of before the *locatio civitatis*. An evident reminder of the 13th century church is the characteristic bend in the axis in relation to the Market Place. St. Mary's Church, like many other Polish churches, went through various phases of building. At the turn of the 13th and 14th centuries the second of the brick-built churches was put up, traces of which can be found in the present edifice. It was probably consecrated in 1320. The third church on the same site began to be built after the middle of the 14th century. It was founded by 42 a Cracow councillor Mikołaj Wierzynek. At the end of the 14th century a stained glass window was put in the presbytery, which has remained to this very day. Also at the same time (1392—97), the builder Mikołaj Werner put up the slender two-aisle main basilica of the church. In the years 1435—46 the chapels designed by the architect Franciszek Wiechoń were built. When, in 1442, the vaulting of the presbytery collapsed, a new stellar one was put up by the builder Czipser. Finally, in 1478, the higher of the two towers was crowned with a particularly harmonious spire with a characteristic pointed top, surrounded with a wreath of little spires. This spire, the work of the carpenter Mateusz Heringk, has become part of the landscape of Cracow, becoming one of the symbols of the city. In the 17th century, the spire was adorned with a gilded crown, a symbol of the Mother of God, the patron saint of the church. The monumental St. Mary's Church, with its two characteristic towers, is a dominant part in the composition of the Market Place. Only the Town Hall Tower on the other side of the Market Place can match it, towering high above the other buildings.

In the first half of the 15th century, the 13th century churches of the Dominicans and the Franciscans were rebuilt. The Dominican Church was changed into a basilica of the Cracow type, with a modest brick façade crowned by a gable ornamented with the coats of arms of the benefactors of the Order. Gabled chapels were built onto the aisles. The cloisters connected with the Romanesque church and the monastery chapter-house were also built in the 14th century. The numerous epitaphs and pictures mostly come from the Renaissance and Baroque periods. The pillars between the nave and aisles and the Gothic vaulting were reconstructed after the great fire of Cracow in 1850. On the other hand, the Franciscan Church was enlarged (1436), a main nave was built and a many-sided apse was added to the presbytery. The cloisters were also built about this time.

Speaking of Gothic architecture in Cracow, mention is due also to the monumental churches of Kazimierz, neighbouring Cracow to the south. In this royal town, not long after the *locatio civitatis* (1335), the building was started of two large basilicas: St. Catherine's Church (Augustinian) and the parish church of Corpus Christi. The building of the Augustinian Church was initiated before the middle of the century by King Casimir the Great. A considerable contribution was made towards the foundation of the monastery and the church by the powerful Lanckoroński family. In 1378 the consecration took place of the long and slender presbytery, surrounded by buttresses. The building of the basilical church, which according to the original plan was supposed to be more than a dozen metres longer, was finished before the end of the 14th century. On the north side of the church there were cloisters and the chapels of St. Thomas and St. Dorothea, built before the consecration of the presbytery. Both of the chapels have the characteristic architectural features of the epoch of Casimir the Great — the first of them is supported by one pillar and the other by two pillars. In the chapel of St. Thomas (which is now the vestry) there is some writing on the keystones of the vaulting, which says: *Ka-zy-mir*[us], referring to King Casimir the Great, the founder of St. Catherine's Church. The slender proportions of the brickwork in St. Catherine's Church are striking, and so are the many-sided apse of the presbytery and the buttresses crowned with their beautiful pinnacles. Limestone was used for the details. The result was a slender, ornamental building, in which the stone work contrasted excellently with the brickwork, giving a really beautiful artistic effect. The interior, with is white plaster finish, has rather severe but excellent proportions. The stellar vaulting in the presbytery was done circa 1505 by the builder Hanusz. The previous vaulting was destroyed during the earthquake that rocked Cracow in 1443.

The building of the Corpus Christi Church was started by a royal foundation in c. 1340. It was supervised by the Czipser family of architects from Kazimierz. The presbytery was completed in the years 1369—87 and later, work was started on the body of the basilica. Ladislaus Jagiełło entrusted the church to the care of the Canons Regular of the Lateran brought by the king from Kłodzko in 1405. Towards the end of the 15th century a façade gable was added, but the tower was only put up in the second half of the 16th century and in the 17th century it was crowned with an early Baroque spire. The Corpus Christi Church is a prolonged two-aisle basilica with a many-sided apse. From the north, a two-floor oratory, which is higher than the aisle and looks like a transept, adds a little variety to the church. The church of today is given character by the Baroque altars which go very well with the Gothic interior.

Of the other Gothic churches in Cracow, mention is due to the charming little Church of the Holy Cross, once linked with the order of the Holy Ghost Fathers. The rectangular presbytery built of crude stone is dated about 1300. The square nave was completed a hundred years later and is supported by one pillar, from which the clusters of ribs supporting the vaulting branch out.

At the same time as St. Mary's Church was built, another small brick Church of St. Barbara (1394—1402) was also put up. St. Barbara's underwent various reconstructions in the following centuries so that its Gothic character has all but disappeared. At the turn of the 15th and 16th centuries, a picturesque openwork chapel was built onto the façade covered with late Gothic ornamention.

After the fire that destroyed the Romanesque castle in 1306, Ladislaus the Short started the reconstruction of Wawel Hill. It was then that the tower named after him was built, parts of which have remained to this day in the walls of the Renaissance palace. Casimir the Great, wishing to preserve the relics of the earlier Romanesque structures, erected some new buildings round a rather irregular courtyard. To this very day you can see in the north wing a chamber dating back to the first half of the 14th century, with the vaulting supported by a single pillar. During the reign of Jadwiga and Jagiełło, a tower that was called the Danish Tower, with characteristic stone decoration formed by the interlacing of arches and strapwork, was put up by Ladislaus the Short's tower. It is distinguished today for its elegance and refinement and is an excellent example of courtly art. Next to it is a mediaeval "belvedere", which bears the name of the Hen's Leg Tower.

The Hen's Leg Tower and the Danish Tower create a picturesque accent in the eastern part of the royal castle on Wawel Hill.

Lay building was much more modest than sacral building in the 14th and 15th centuries. Taking advantage of the years of peace and prosperity, Casimir the Great also erected municipal and private buildings. In the middle of the 14th century the Cloth Hall finally took shape. It was a long brick-built hall covered with a roof, with the shops situated at the sides. Cloth Hall lasted in this shape till the middle of the 16th century. On both sides of Cloth Hall there were pottery, fish, ironware and other stalls. It was a trading centre. Here all the life and business of the burghers was concentrated. Here also all the important state ceremonies took place, honoured by the attendance of the monarch. On the day after his coronation, the king went to the Market Place with his retinue for the people to pay him homage. Next to Cloth Hall and the three hundred stalls, there were also the municipal weighing house, the Town Hall and the pillory in the Market Place.

Among the oldest mediaeval buildings of the city was the Town Hall, which was a landmark in the panorama of the city because of its high tower. It was the object of special care for the burghers, a symbol of the glory and power of their city. So attention was given to the design and artistic form of the Town Hall. The first mention of the Cracow Town Hall comes from the beginning of the 14th century. In 1383 the slender tower was already standing. It was once crowned with a spire like the one on St. Mary's Church, which was replaced in 1686 by a Baroque spire, the work of Piotr Beber. The Town Hall was demolished at the beginning of the 19th century.

The third big mediaeval building, apart from the Town Hall and Cloth Hall, was the Collegium Maius of the Jagiellonian University. Purchased towards the end of the 14th century, the building was enlarged and reconstructed. In the middle of the 15th century the Stuba Communis was built and decorated with bay windows, like the ones in the Charles University in Prague. It was not until 1493 that the university buildings were linked together to form one whole round the arcaded courtyard. Gathered together on 1 May 1493 the professors of the Almae Matris decided "in the presence of and with the unanimous agreement of all those entitled to vote and take decisions... that the Collegium Maius, unexpectedly burnt down and damaged, should be rebuilt in a beautiful shape, not only to make it a dignified building for common use, but also to renovate those parts of the building where the violent fire had destroyed or badly damaged it". At this time. Master Jan designed the steps and the gallery running round the courtyard. In the years 1507—09, the 44 assembly hall was built, under the supervision of the builder Marek. Finally, in the years 1515—19, the masters Benedykt and Stefan built the spacious library (*Libraria*). Today, the Collegium Maius is a large building with distinct gables and a small oriel, which add some variety to the façade, the accents of which are the small stone windows and the large Renaissance windows, which light the Assembly Hall and the Library. The courtyard, with its Gothic arcade, is one of the romantic corners of Cracow. Its character is decided by the cut of the pillars supporting the gothic arcade, which is covered by crystal vaulting. In olden times the professors lived in Collegium Maius and there were lecture rooms there; today it is the seat of the Museum of the Jagiellonian University. Nearby the Collegium Maius, the Collegium Minus and numerous dormitories for students were built.

It would be difficult to describe the houses of the burghers because with the passing of years they have lost their original character. Probably in the 13th century, scattered building predominated and there were not many brick-built houses. The expansion of Cracow mostly took place in the 14th century and at the beginning of the 15th century. The houses of the wealthiest burghers were built round the Market Place and also in Floriańska, Sławkowska, Grodzka, and Szewska Streets. They stood right next to each other, connected by two-floor façades crowned with brick gables. Limestone was used for building the details, such as richly carved portal frames, and also vaulting ribs and pillars. In some of the houses, mainly in the Market Place, vaulted chambers have survived (House At the Rams, Grey House, Hetman's House and the Salamanders House) and also some Gothic sculptures. Special attention is due to the decoration of the ground-floor hall in the Hetman's House. The houses of Cracow had water laid on; this is mentioned in documents from the end of the 14th century, and the streets were paved with cobblestones.

Gothic municipal fortifications in Cracow have remained. They were built gradually from the 13th to the 15th century. In the earliest period (13th —14th centuries) stone walls and seven gates were built; later turrets were built and in 1575 there were 33 of them. During the 15th century a bulwark was built, that is, a lower rampart defending access to the main fortifications, and at the end of the century the fortification unit by the Florian Gate was additionally strengthened. In the years 1498—99, the most valuable example of defence building — the Barbican — was built. It was put up because of the constant threat from the Turks. The large, round brick-built Barbican with its bristling turrets with their pointed spires, is a characteristic feature of that side of the city. It was once joined to the Florian Gate by walls, making one whole defence unit. At the beginning of the 19th century the defence walls were pulled down and replaced with the Planty Gardens, where one can take a walk round the town; but the fortification unit by the Florian Gate with the Barbican, and also the 15th century turrets, the Haberdashers', Joiners' and Carpenters' turrets, were all saved. This preserved part of the old defences, with a city gate, walls and the Barbican, gives an idea as to what the mediaeval fortifications looked like.

Apart from the parts of the old city walls that have survived there are also four Gothic towers which were part of the defences of Wawel Hill, the Lubranka, Senators', Sandomierz and Thieves' towers which together with the later fortifications, create a strong defence accent on Wawel Hill.

The mediaeval buildings of Cracow are enhanced by sculptures and mural paintings, which make one integral whole. There are many examples of Gothic sculpture that well represent the high level of this art, but above all, the monumental royal tombs in the cathedral are decisive in establishing the character of Cracow sculpture in the Middle Ages.

The picture opens with the tomb of Ladislaus the Short (d. 1333); then come the tombs of Casimir the Great (d. 1370), Ladislaus Jagiełło (d. 1434) and Casimir IV (d. 1492). Each of them consists of a rectangular box, on which a bas-relief was placed, showing what the deceased monarch looked like. On each tomb there was a canopy supported by columns. The sides of the tomb were filled with bas-reliefs showing people weeping at the death of the monarch. On the sarcophagus of Casimir IV and Ladislaus Jagiełło, the weepers are holding shields with the coats of arms of the Polish Kingdom and the Grand Duchy of Lithuania. The sarcophagus of Ladislaus the Short, made of stone and very severe in form, is striking for the beautifully modelled head of the monarch. A masterpiece of mediaeval sculpture is the marble monument to Casimir the Great. It was founded by Louis of Hungary, the successor to the deceased and his nephew, and it was made by artists brought from abroad, who were familiar with the Austrian art of those times. An exceptional work of art is the sarcophagus of Ladislaus Jagiełło, carved in the first quarter of the 15th century. The incomparable artistic form separates it from all Polish art of the Middle Ages. It is carved out of red marble, covered with a 16th century Renaissance canopy and creates a uniform whole, rather reminiscent of Italian sculptures of the quattrocento period. Scholars suggest that the artists who sculpted the sarcophagus of Jagiełło were well acquainted with the Renaissance art of Florence of the beginning of the 15th century. This would account for the unrepeatable and incomparable artistic form of the tomb.

The last of the fully Gothic royal monuments was the sarcophagus of Casimir IV, sculpted from mottled Salzburg marble. There is the date 1492 — and what is even more important — the signature and the hallmark of the artist, in this case Wit Stwosz (Veit Stoss). The shape of the monument is similar to those described above. Wit Stwosz was helped in this work by Jorg Huber of Passau, who sculpted the capitals of the columns supporting the canopy, showing the story of the salvation of man. The sarcophagus of Casimir IV is a work of art of exceptionally high class. The reason for this was the great artistic individuality of the man who created it, Wit Stwosz, the most outstanding European sculptor at the end of the Middle Ages.

Cracow was famous for its excellent wood-carvers. The best examples of this art are the Madonna of Krużlowa (which is kept in the National Museum in Cracow) and the Pietà in the Church of St. Barbara. Towards the end of the 15th century, the burghers of Cracow were famous for the main altar that they had sculpted for St. Mary's Church and which cost 2,808 florins, a sum equal to a year's city budget. The altar in St. Mary's Church became a monument to the sponsorship and the culture of the burghers of mediaeval Cracow. The sculpting of the altar was done by Master Wit Stwosz, who came from Nuremberg to carry out this commission and stayed in Cracow from 1477 to 1496. He was surrounded with care by the municipal authorities and exempted from the payment of dues to the city. Master Wit lived through the most creative years of his career in Cracow. For 12 years, with intervals, he worked on the altar for St. Mary's Church (1477—89). This, the largest polyptych to be found in Europe, consists of a central panel with an expressive scene showing the Dormition of the Mother of God, and four wing panels with bas-relief scenes from the life of Christ. In the predella the artist has sculpted the family tree of Jesse with the genealogy of Jesus Christ. The altar-piece is a masterpiece of figural sculpture. The centre panel shows the real drama of the apostles present at the death of the Madonna. They are undergoing true depths of emotion, which can be seen in the expressions of real pain on their faces. How different the Madonna looks, having accepted the will of God, who has called her to eternal life. Her face, full of serenity, is in direct contrast with the faces of the apostles. In harmony with the tension-filled atmosphere surrounding the death of Mary, the folds of the robes are twisted tortuously and there are strong contrasts of light and shade. The whole altar-piece emanates gold light which covers the robes of those taking part in the drama happening in the panel. The sculptor has mastered his material faultlessly. Dynamism, pathos, monumentality, agitation — these are surely the *mots justes* to describe the style of the altar-piece in St. Mary's Church and also the style of Wit Stwosz. Apart from the well-known works (the altarpiece in St. Mary's Church, the tomb of Casimir IV) Wit Stwosz also sculpted a very expressive Crucified Christ in an aisle of St. Mary's. He also designed a plaque for the outstanding humanist Filippo Buonaccorsi (d. 1496), which was placed in the Dominican Church. It was cast in bronze in the workshop of Peter Vischer in Nuremberg, where Wit Stwosz went in 1496 and spent the rest of his life. He died in Nuremberg in 1533. He was the most outstanding European sculptor of the late Middle Ages. He gathered numerous pupils around him in Cracow and the workshop of the artist soon won fame all over Little Poland. The style of Stwosz had a major influence on sculpting in Cracow in the first half of the 16th century. Sculpture strongly influenced by Stwosz for a considerable time represented a trend parallel to Renaissance art.

Monumental murals were painted in Cracow towards the end of the 14th century. The murals in the cloisters of the monastery of the Augustinians have been preserved in good condition, and so have those in the monastery of the Franciscans, but the scenes of the Passion in the Holy Cross Church have unfortunately deteriorated. As regards the time they were painted and the style, they 46 are uniform. They were painted in the first half of the 15th century and reveal a connection with Bohemian painting, although creatively transformed. We can also see Polish-Bohemian artistic connections in sculpture, architecture and in the painting of miniatures. The influence of the court culture of the epoch of the Emperor Charles IV could be clearly seen in Polish art, a proof of numerous artistic contacts.

The most beautiful and excellent in the formal sense are the murals in the cloisters of the monastery of the Franciscans. From the artistic point of view they are very much better than the other polychromes there. Among the most valuable are the very lyrical and delicate Annunciation and the Stigmatization of St. Francis. They both show a very strong Italian influence. Also worthy of mention is Our Lady of Consolation at the Augustinian Church, which was repainted at the beginning of the 16th century.

An exception among the Cracow murals is the "Ruthenian" polychrome that covers the Holy Cross Chapel at Wawel Cathedral. Both the chapel and the paintings were completed in 1470. They were founded by Queen Elizabeth of Habsburg and King Casimir IV. Most of them show scenes from the Gospel. They provide an excellent example of the artistic tastes of the king, the son of Ladislaus Jagiełło and the Ruthenian Princess Sophia. There was a good reason for Jan Długosz writing that Ladislaus Jagiełło "decorated the churches at Wiślica, Sandomierz and Gniezno with Greek paintings". Casimir IV inherited and continued his father's tastes and interests, bringing artists from distant Pskov. He entrusted the painting of the polychrome in the Holy Cross Chapel to thme.

There is no doubt that Cracow took the first place as regards painting on wood. About 1400 an extremely vital painters' guild was formed there, and from the beginning of the 15th century these painters began the production of pictures on religious subjects, which were painted on linden wood covered with a gesso coating, sometimes richly gilded. A characteristic feature of the Cracow school in the second half of the 15th century, were the large triptychs painted in a very realistic style. The earliest of these, called the Dominican painting, was done just after 1460 and consists of over a dozen compartments with scenes from the Passion and Marian scenes, very realistically painted and full of drama. Quite different, both as regards subject and form, is the Holy Trinity Triptych painted in 1467 in the Holy Cross Chapel. It consists of a carved panel with a figure representing the Holy Trinity and figures of the Holy Virgins: Catherine, Barbara, Dorothea and Margaret. On the wings there are scenes from the lives of the saints seen against landscapes: St. George, St. Paul, St. Secundus and St. Eustachius. And in addition there are choirs of prophets, holy virgins, apostles and martyrs, all of whom are singing the praises of the Creator. This is one of the outstanding works of the Cracow school of painting and sculpture.

The poetic scenes from the life of Christ in the Augustinian triptych, painted in the second half of the 15th century, testify to the outstanding talent of their supposed author, Mikołaj Haberschrack, who very skilfully used his colours and was a master of lyrical landscapes, particularly evident in the panel showing Christ in Gethsemane. Skill in operating with a large scale of colours was one of the features of Cracow painting in the second half of the 15th century. In the Triptych of Our Lady of Sorrow in Cracow Cathedral considerable Netherlandish influences can be seen. It was founded by Elizabeth of Habsburg and this is confirmed by the coat of arms of the Habsburgs. Like the Triptych of the Holy Trinity it is a carved panel with painted lateral panels showing scenes from the life of Christ. Among the characters portrayed the faces of Casimir the Great and Ladislaus Jagiełło can be discerned, which testifies to the far advanced realism of Cracow painting.

According to surviving written sources, churches in the whole of the once large diocese purchased paintings. Only very modest remnants are left today of the very impressive work of the Cracow painters, but these give a good idea of the creative possibilities, the quality and subject matter of the paintings produced. The National Museum in Cracow has quite a lot of them.

The Middle Ages are worthily closed by the very large polyptych devoted to St. John the
Almoner (about 1502) with its ingenious folding system, which is on the borderline of Gothic and

Renaissance art. The technical excellence and compositional impetus of this work are striking. On the lateral panels of the polyptych the artist presents the legend of St. John the Almoner comparing his life with the lives of other hermits. The sharp folds of the drapery of the robes and the gold background belong to the Gothic period, but the light and bright colours, making the landscape a really modern one, are already an introduction to Renaissance art.

Mediaeval Cracow was famous for its well organized artistic craftsmanship. This gave the capital of the Polish state the lead as a centre of goldsmithery in Europe. During the reign of Casimir the Great the goldsmiths' guild was formed and the works produced by its members are now the most treasured possessions of churches and museums. The chalices endowed by Casimir the Great for the churches at Trzemeszno (1351), Stopnica (1362), and Kalisz (1363) and the royal crown were all made by members of the guild. They are distinguished by their elegant shape, the subtle workmanship and the use of the motif of the stylized lily. Gothic monstrances were also made in Cracow in the middle of the 15th century, for example, the monstrances in Luborzyca (1470) and Wieliczka (1490). In the treasury of St. Mary's Church there are some unique Gothic chalices, which date from the 15th century and the beginning of the 16th century. Two exceptionally costly works of goldsmithery are the reliquaries for the head of St. Stanislaus (in the Cathedral Treasury). They are many-sided in shape. The older one was offered by Queen Sophia, the fourth wife of Ladislaus Jagiełło, during the coronation ceremony (1424). It was shortly to be replaced by a richer reliquary. In 1504, Queen Elizabeth of Habsburg presented to the Cathedral a pure gold reliquary for the head of St. Stanislaus, made by the court goldsmith Marcin Marciniec. On the sides there are bas-relief scenes from the life of St. Stanislaus, and the cover is wholly studded with sapphires, pearls and diamonds, with a unique black diamond among them. Marcin Marciniec also made the sceptre of Cardinal Frederick, which was presented by the latter to the University. It is today one of the most ornamental items in the University treasury.

The most beautiful Polish mediaeval embroidery is also connected with the cult of St. Stanislaus, namely the chasuble offered to the Cathedral in 1504 by the Voivode Piotr Kmita. It features scenes from the legend of St. Stanislaus embroidered in relief. It would be impossible to mention all the relics of artistic handicrafts that are still to be found in the treasuries and museums of Cracow, and the inventory of the Cathedral Treasury, compiled in 1563, is a proof of the wealth of the churches. It mentions 300 liturgical objects, 150 candlesticks and nearly 600 rich fabrics, among which chasubles, copes and dalmatics predominated. They were donated to the church by the kings and the clergy. Other Cracow churches were given similar gifts by the burghers, who were very generous in this respect.

At the end of the 15th century, Cracow was already a fully-fledged city, the capital of the great state of the Jagiellons. The culture of Cracow radiated to neighbouring territories, making this beautiful city one of the main European cultural centres. And this is how the "Mediaeval Autumn" ended for Cracow.

CHAPTER III · CRACOVIA TOTIUS POLONIAE URBS CELEBERRIMA

CRACOW IN THE DAYS OF THE LAST JAGIELLONS

The balance of the history of Poland during the reign of Casimir IV (1447—92) proved favourable from the political, economic and cultural points of view. The year 1466 brought the end of the thirteen years' war with the Order of the Teutonic Knights. By virtue of the Peace of Toruń (1466) the Grand Master of the Order recognized Polish suzerainty and, what is more, the lost lands, including Gdańsk Pomerania and Warmia, were regained by Poland. The Kingdom of Poland gained access to the Baltic Sea, which in the years that followed brought a very quick economic development, mainly of the towns situated on the Vistula, including Cracow. This political influence of the Jagiellons in the second half of the 15th century reached ever deeper into Europe. In 1471, Ladislaus II gained the Bohemian throne. In 1490, he gained the Hungarian throne too. Thus the countries ruled by the Jagiellonian dynasty included Poland, the Grand Duchy of Lithuania, Bohemia, Moravia, Silesia and Hungary. Together they formed a powerful political entity and a vital cultural organism. Cracow also had many kinds of contacts with Buda and Prague. This was when Cracow came under the influence of humanism. In the years 1491—95 Nicolaus Copernicus studied at the Cracow Academy. It is thought that the nucleus of his heliocentric conception was born here, within the walls of the Cracow Academy.

Handicrafts developed too. The number of craftsmen's guilds grew in comparison with the 15th century, reaching the number of about 40 in the 16th century. This had the influence of growing specialization, making it essential to divide craftsmen so far united in one guild into separate guilds. The number of artistic workshops also grew: in the first half of the 16th century in Cracow, there were over 100 bricklaying and stonework workshops, 100 goldsmiths' workshops and about 80 painting workshops. At the same time, the development of the economy demanded new forms of production. There was a large number of craftsmen working outside the guilds, who represented keen competition to those united in the guilds. They were called *a parte* workers, after the Latin expression, which means "on the side". Both local trade and foreign trade developed. Every Tuesday and Friday the local peasants used to come from the surrounding villages to the Market Place in their carts to sell their goods. The colourful picture of life in the Cracow Market Place cannot be better presented than in the descriptions of the contemporary poet Mikołaj Rej:

"If you would like to see how the poor eat, go to the Cracow Market Place and you will be surprised: how one of the women is frying sausages, another is selling gruel, yet another is selling baked liver with vinegar and onions... yet another runs round the Market Place with wafers, and another with wreaths, yet another sits and tries to sell herbs and red ointment. So the cereal seller, the herring, the butter, the candle, the glass, the apple sellers, the grinder, the boot seller, the fishmonger, the sour soup seller, the beetroot soup seller, the man selling cucumbers, are all sitting there... who would be able to count them all!" Merchants from Hungary, Ruthenia, Bohemia and Silesia all came to Cracow. From 1589 the city took tariffs for goods brought to the city and taken out of it. The tariff books kept in the city archives form an excellent guide to the trade contacts Cracow had with the whole world. The first half of the 16th century is a period of the greatest economic and cultural development of Cracow.

In the 16th century, Poland had a population of about 10 million, while Cracow had a population of about 20,000, who lived in the city itself and in the suburbs and the independent neighbouring towns of Kazimierz, Kleparz and Garbary. Situated far from the wars with Muscovy, the Tartars and Valachians, Cracow lived a quiet and prosperous life, free from the upheavals which took place in the eastern and southeastern parts of the state.

Cracow remained the seat of the monarchy, and also, because of this, the witness of the greatest events in the history of the Polish state. It was in Cracow that the treaty which finally regulated the relations between the Teutonic Knights and Poland was signed in 1525. By virtue of the provisions of the treaty, the Order was secularized. The secular Prussian State (Ducal Prussia), which owed fealty to the Polish crown, was ruled by Prince Albert. On 10 April 1525, the Cracow Market Place witnessed the ceremony of the act of homage, whereby Albert Hohenzollern publicly recognized the suzerainty of the Polish King Sigismund (I) the Old. According to a contemporary poet, Andrzej Krzycki, the ceremony was exceptionally magnificent: "On that day, at dawn, a framework was built by the Town Hall and covered with cloth of gold, especially in the higher place, the so-called majestic place, where the king and his son were to sit. Crowds of people came into the Market Place. All the streets where the procession was going to march were lined with armed men, and everyone tried to appear either in magnificent robes or well armed. His Majesty was surrounded by a large and splendid suite of senators and nobles... They were followed by the Queen with the prince, her son, and the princesses and a great suite of eminent ladies, in beautiful carriages and coaches. The King went into the Town Hall and the Queen went with her suite to a house opposite, from where it would be possible to view the ceremony that was about to take place... When the King had taken his place on the throne, first came the Bishop of Pomerania and numerous councillors and subjects of Prince Albert... and having delivered beautiful speeches, they asked that the King should look graciously upon his nephew Prince Albert and give him the lands and property in fief and to make Albert a vassal of the Polish crown. Soon afterwards came Prince Albert with two princes (George and Frederick) and delivered a speech of almost the same subject matter, ensuring the King of his exceptional faithfulness, humility and dependence. Answering speeches were then made to the councillors and to the Prince himself, after which Father Piotr Tomicki made a spirited speech of elegant style in Latin... Afterwards the Prince went up to the throne and the King's feet and kneeling there received the banner with a black eagle crowned with the letter 'S' on its breast, and the King spoke the words making him the owner of the Duchy and lands in Prussia that had been specified in the Treaty. Next, taking the banner, with which he [Albert] also touched his brother George as his nearest successor, he made an oath with his hand on the book of the Gospel." Several dozen years later, after the conclusion of the Polish-Lithuanian Union in Lublin (1569), Cracow became the capital of the extensive Commonwealth of Two Nations. But even before this, suites of envoys were to be seen in the streets of the city, and ceremonious entries of bishops and also royal entries into the city were made. In 1518, Cracovians viewed the pompous entry of the Italian princess Bona Sforza, who was the bride of King Sigismund (I) the Old. The contemporary historian Marcin Bielski gives the following account of this memorable event:

"This [year] Bona, the Queen of Sigismund, was brought to Cracow on 15 April and the King went to meet his bride in the company of the dukes of Masovia and other nobles who were his counsellors and they put up tents outside the city and waited for her there; when the Queen alighted from her horse, she was met first by Archbishop Łaski and afterwards the King came out of his tent, and having greeted her led her into the tent (red carpets were everywhere on the ground); there all the eminent people who had come with the Queen greeted the King, and then they all went in the direction of the city. And all this time salvoes were being fired from big guns and some of the soldiers were firing their rifles, others were tilting with each other. After this, before the sun set, they went into the church, where Piotr Tomicki with his coat of arms of Łodzia, Bishop of Przemyśl and vice-chancellor, greeted the Queen in the name of the canons. She then left the church for the palace and on the fourth day, on Sunday, she was crowned." The Italian queen brought with her a large number of her fellow countrymen; in the first half of the 16th century, at the royal court, in the diplomatic service and in the church hierarchy, there were nearly 260 Italians. From that time, apart from the large German group, the number of Italians began to grow too. With the inflow of Italians, the economic and cultural contacts of Cracow with Italy were enlivened. Queen Bona was followed by numerous courtiers from Florence, Bologna and Milan. The Italians not only strengthened the royal court, but also the merchant class. They soon became bankers (the Montelupi, the Cellari and the Soderini families). They were very quickly Polonized. They formed a separate confraternity at the Franciscan monastery. It was thanks to this group of Italians that Renaissance art spread and consolidated in Poland. They were largely responsible for the tone of artistic culture in the first half of the 16th century. Cracow also owes its postal communication to the Italian who arrived there. By royal charter (1558), the merchant Prosper Provano became the organizer of the Polish post. Later the Montelupi family took over. The post linked Cracow with Venice.

Apart from the Italians, numerous Germans also arrived in Cracow, mainly from Silesia, Lusatia and the Alsace-Lorraine border (the Boner and the Decius families). Having settled in the capital of Poland, they quickly made admirable careers, for instance Jan Boner (d. 1523), minister of the treasury to King Sigismund I, burgrave of the Royal Castle on Wawel Hill. The successor to Jan Boner was his nephew Seweryn (d. 1549), who managed to enter the magnate circles. The Boners were rich bankers, like the Chigi family in Italy and the Fugger family in Germany. The newly arrived families were quickly Polonized.

An evident sign of the full Polonization of Cracow was the restoration in St. Mary's Church of services in the Polish language in 1537. Until then the Polish population had to go to the small Church of St. Barbara and other churches of Cracow, while in the parish church the sermon was delivered in the German language. It was only in the fourth decade of the 16th century that things were changed. The increase of the Polish population, the slow Polonization of the municipal council, caused a "war" for a Polish service in St. Mary's Church. The king issued a decree saying that the German sermon was not to be longer heard in St. Mary's but was to be transferred to St. Barbara's Church. The king's decree thus read: "Considering it to be an affront to the people of Polish origin that a foreign language should be given priority in the city and in the best of our churches, and knowing that the Polish population belonging to that parish has multiplied to such an extent that they can no longer hear sermons in the chapel of St. Barbara, once filled to the brim with listeners and which can now no longer hold them all, causing a lot of humiliation to members of the Polish nation and at the same time many dangers, particularly in an unnecessary crowd of people, ... we would like to put an end to this with our decree, which we would like to be regarded as final."

From the time of the decree, the Polish language became prevalent. It can be found in the municipal records with increasing frequency next to the Latin language.

Sixteenth century Cracow was the main centre of Polish learning. The high standards of scholarship, the reception of humanism and the patronage of the king, gave the Academy in Cracow an international character. The activity of the Academy at the end of the 15th century was generally known in Europe and highly esteemed. The astronomical sciences flourished. Jan of Głogów (c. 1445—1507) and Wojciech of Brudzewo (c. 1446—95) developed this field of science and trained many students. In 1493 Hartmann Schedel, the well known humanist of Nuremberg, wrote about the Cracow Academy that: "There is no other university as famous in the whole of Germany as regards astronomy." The theory of Copernicus was taught in Cracow by Joachim Retyk (1545—72), Walenty Fontana (1545—1618) and Jan Brożek (1585—1652). At the same time studies were carried on in the fields of geography and cartography, and interest was also shown in geographical discoveries (Jan of Głogów and Jan of Stobnica). Maciej of Miechów, the outstanding physician, historian and geographer, wrote *Tractatus de duabus Sarmatiis* (1517) which won him fame in this respect, for it gave a description of the lands between the Vistula and the Don, and the Caspian Sea. The same scholar also wrote a history of Poland (*Chronica Polonorum*). Botany served medicine; medical uses of plants were studied. Szymon of Łowicz, a professor of the Almae Matris, compiled a Polish botanical dictionary (1532). A systematic study of herbs was made by the Cracow scholar Marcin of Urzędów (d. 1573), the author of the first Polish herbal (*Herbarz polski, to jest o przyrodzeniu ziół,* 1595).

In the years 1500—60, there were 12,000 students attending the Cracow Academy, of whom a large percentage were foreign students from Hungary, Slovakia, Brandenburg, Lusatia, Saxony, Prussia and Bavaria. About the middle of the 16th century the development of the university was violently checked. There were many reasons for this. The Reformation caused a religious split from 1517 and foreign and Polish students were drawn away from the Cracow Academy to newly set up universities of various faiths (Wittenberg, Frankfurt on the Odra, Königsberg). At the same time, professors who favoured the Reformation had to leave the Cracow Academy. The unchecked development of humanism in foreign universities attracted the gentry. The young noblemen ever more frequently chose to study at Italian, German, French and Swiss universities.

It should be pointed out here that, in the 16th century, the gentry had gained a position of decisive importance in the Polish state. In order to become a church dignitary or occupy an important state post, young noblemen no longer had to have academic degrees, as had previously been required. In spite of this, the Cracow Academy opened new departments in the first half of the 16th century: in 1518 Rudolf Agricola took charge of the Department of Rhetoric, also the fashionable Greek and Hebrew languages were taught there too. All the brilliance of the Cracow Almae Matris was recorded by the English humanist Leonard Coxe in his printed speech *De laudibus Academiae Cracoviensis* (1517). The poets Mikołaj Rej and Jan Kochanowski attended the university and so did the writers Andrzej Frycz Modrzewski and Stanisław Orzechowski, as well as the well known historians, Marcin Kromer, Maciej Stryjkowski, Świętosław Orzelski and Bartosz Paprocki. The university was able to resist the hegemony of the Jesuits, who from the end of the 16th century were stubbornly trying to master the schools in Poland and impose an alien system of education on them. In the long-lasting campaign (1578—1634) the Cracow Academy was able to defend itself and resist the efforts that were made to open higher monastery schools in Cracow.

The social system in Cracow did not undergo any major changes from the Middle Ages. The people who had the right to live there were divided into three groups:

> *ordo senatorius* (councillors)
> *ordo scabinorum et mercantorum* (assessors and merchants)
> *ordo mechanicorum* (craftsmen).

The last two groups formed the so-called commoners, who were constantly fighting for power with the municipal council, which represented the social élite and economic might. Those inhabitants of the city who did not have municipal rights were the plebeians. They were a dangerous element in the fight for power. The city was governed by a municipal council of 24 councillors (*consules praesidentes*) who were elected for life. The council was made up of representatives of the wealthiest burgher families. The commoners raised a sharp protest against the licence of the councillors. As a result of these struggles and disputes, Sigismund I called an office of forty men into being (*quadriginti viri*), which represented the commoners and mainly controlled the financial activity of the municipal council. At the end of the 16th century, when the income of the city did not cover the budget outlays, the power of the commoners increased, as, in the event of a shortage of money, the municipal council was forced to tax them. The whole of the 16th century witnessed a constant struggle in Cracow for the democratization of power.

THE REFORMATION IN CRACOW

Apart from political events, colourful processions of envoys and royalty, university and social problems, Cracow also witnessed major religious changes, which affected the life of the city. The pronouncements of Luther (1517), the activities of Zwingli and Calvin, had strong effect on the Cracow humanists, particularly in university circles, which followed the developments in Germany with great interest. Luther's books were quickly sold — and publicly at that — in the Academy. People eagerly read about all the religious innovations. The relevant publications were brought to Cracow by merchants, students studying at foreign universities and political and religious emigrés coming there from Germany. Luther's books were propagated very quickly and with equal speed war was declared on them. However, the strict edicts issued by King Sigismund I in 1520, 1522, 1523, and 1535, aimed against the followers of Lutheranism, did not help much, just as the ban on studying at Wittenberg, where Luther lectured, did not prevent people going there. In Cracow the German burghers quickly accepted the heretic slogans. The seed fell on fertile ground. In answer to this, the bishop's court filed ever more cases of heresy. It was forbidden under the threat of excommunication to read heretic literature. Commissions were even formed to observe bookshops and printing houses. Representatives of the bishop's curia together with delegates from the municipal council were free to search houses and shops for Luther's books. In the records of the bishop's court, numerous cases of heresy can be found. The first names of Luther's followers appeared and then, later, of Calvin's followers. The trial of Katarzyna of the Zalaszowski family, wife of the goldsmith Melchior Weigel, was one of the sensational ones. Not quite ten years after her first trial, this eighty-year-old woman again stood before the bishop's court. The accused denied the divine nature of Jesus Christ and existence of the Holy Trinity. She was sentenced to death, to be burnt at the stake. This event was related as follows by the contemporary writer Łukasz Górnicki:

"At this time, the wife of Melchior, a Cracow burgher, an eighty-year-old woman of the Jewish faith, was burnt at the stake in the Cracow Market Place, and I saw this. There were gathered there at the court of Father Gamrat, Bishop of Cracow, all the canons and collegiates, to hear her profession of faith. When she was asked if she believed in Almighty God, the creator of heaven and earth, she answered: I believe in the God who created everything, what we see and what we do not see; which human understanding cannot fathom, and his goodness fills us, human beings and all the things in the world. She then continued to expand on this for quite a long time, describing the power of God and his inexpressible goodness. Then more questions were put to her: Do you believe in the only son of God, Jesus Christ, who was begotten by the Holy Ghost, etc. Her reply to this was: God had no wife and no son, and did not need them, the only people who need sons are those that die, but God is eternal, and as he was not born, he cannot die. He has us for his sons and his sons are those who go his ways. Here the collegiates cried: You poor woman, you don't speak the truth, be careful; there are prophesies that God was to send his son to the world, and he was to be crucified for our sins, to unite us, still disobedient sons of Adam, with God Our Father. Doctors spoke to her trying to persuade her to change her testimony, but the more they tried to persuade her, the stronger she was in her beliefs, that God could not be a man and be born. When it became clear that she would not be wooed from her Jewish faith, she was found to be a blasphemer against God and she was sent to the municipal office, and several days later, as I said above, she was burnt at the stake, and she went to her death showing no fear." Fortunately there were not many such strict sentences during the Polish Reformation. Poland, because of her multinational character and the fact that many faiths were represented by her citizens, became a tolerant country. People were only rarely burnt at the stake. The Commonwealth won the name of a paradise for heretics in Europe.

A great impact on the development of the Reformation in Cracow was made by a professor of the Academy, Jakub of Iłża. In the years 1528—35 he gave sermons in the Church of St. Stephen. He told the faithful of Luther's teachings and quickly gained a large congregation of listeners and followers. His pupils sharply criticized the Roman Catholic doctrines and the Church hierarchy. Jakub of Iłża was removed from Cracow by a sentence of the bishop's court. But a lot of his pupils and followers remained there, continuing his work.

A considerable influence on the cultural life of Cracow in the 1540's was exercised by a group of humanists gathering at the home of Andrzej Trzecieski. Learned discussions were held on religious problems, led by the court preacher of Queen Bona, Francesco Lismanino. Such illustrious men as Andrzej Frycz Modrzewski, Jakub Przyłuski and the later primate, Jakub Uchański, attended the meetings at Trzecieski's home. Mikołaj Rej, the outstanding poet, had contacts with this group, as did the political writer Stanisław Orzechowski. All the intellectuals who gathered at Trzecieski's home were under the influence of the writings of Erasmus of Rotterdam, who had numerous contacts by correspondence with Poles. King Sigismund I was one of his correspondents. Among the pupils of Erasmus was the Cracow bishop Andrzej Zebrzydowski (d. 1560) and Jan Boner, who was in favour of the Reformation.

As long as King Sigismund I was alive (d. 1548) all radical attacks on the Church were suppressed. The situation underwent a certain change after the death of the monarch. The death of the king brought the underground Reformation trend to the surface. When Sigismund

Augustus, who was in favour of the new slogans, ascended the throne, the Reformation quickly spread to ever wider circles of the community. People began to speak loudly of bringing the Polish language into liturgical texts, there were demands for the abolition of celibacy and also for the Eucharistic Communion. There were also postulates for the creation in Poland of a national church. With an increasing frequence people were referring to the teachings of Calvin. It was particularly to the taste of the wealthy patriciate. Jan Boner, the son of Seweryn, began to give tone to the new trend of the Reformation. He changed quickly from a follower of Luther into a propagator of Calvinism in Cracow. He put the garden behind the Nicholas Gate at the disposal of those who shared his faith, and they were able to gather there safely for prayers and discussion.

Another outstanding protector of dissenters was Just Ludwik Decjusz, the son of Just Decjusz, a well known historian and secretary to Sigismund I. Dissenters gathered at the estate of Decjusz, situated in Wola, outside Cracow, and in his house in Św. Jana Street. The Cracow believers in the teachings of Luther and Calvin had many powerful protectors. In 1557, they were given a minister, who was the well known and highly esteemed preacher, Paweł of Brzeziny.

In the middle of the 16th century there was a split in the Polish Calvinist movement. There was a sharp campaign between the Calvinists and the Anti-Trinitarians. The scene of these dogmatic disputes was Cracow. In the fire of stubborn arguments carried on in broad-sheets and at synods, the split finally came in 1563. An extreme wing separated itself from the Calvinists, called the Minor Church or the Polish Brethren, in other words, the Arians. The ideology of the Arians was the most radical in the history of the Polish Reformation. They absolutely rejected belief in dogmas, and attacked the dogma of the Holy Trinity with particular fury. Some of them fought belief in the immortality of the human soul and negated the divinity of Christ. They were against the baptism of babies, considering baptism received without consciousness invalid. So they demanded another baptism when the person was an adult. They called for pure apostolic faith, a truly Christian way of life, free of social injustice. They opposed feudal oppression and war. They were in favour of the general availability of work and the duty to work and the just division of goods. The ideology proclaimed by the Polish Brethren was mainly accepted by the plebeian masses. In 1569, the Arians set up their own settlement at Raków and it was there that they had their central base.

But before the Arian community was set up in Raków, the Polish Brethren were mostly concentrated in Cracow and Lublin. Quite a lot of the townspeople were in favour of the new doctrine, mainly craftsmen. One of the leaders of the Arians, Szymon Ronenberg, came from Cracow. An Italian, Faustus Socinus, the leading ideologist of the Polish Brethren, lived in Cracow for ten years. In 1597, he had to flee the town before a crowd of fanatics. Cracow was also the home of the Arian Printing House of Aleksy Rodecki, which was later moved to Raków. The Arians had their house of worship in Szpitalna Street, which was destroyed in 1591. The Polish Brethren, with their plebeian ultrademocratic ideology, play quite an important role in the history of Renaissance Cracow. There is no doubt that they contributed considerably to the ferment among the people who had faiths other than Roman Catholic. With their social attitude they had an appeal for the poor strata of the population.

The quick spread of the activity of the Arians led to an early conciliation and consolidation of the Cracow Calvinist congregation. About 1570 there was a new stabilization of dissidents under the Calvinist flag. In 1572, they purchased a house in Św. Jana Street as a meeting place. Previously a Calvinist school had been founded, of which the French reformer Jean Thenaudus was the director for many years. The Reformation synods had a moralizing effect on the believers in the new religion. They concentrated, above all, on questions of faith and morality. They demanded absolute temperance, fought against luxury articles in dress, as well as stupidity and idleness. They came out against an immoral way of life and rigorous sexual ethics were introduced.

Germans and Italians played quite an important role in the Cracow Reformation. Italians represented the extreme trends. They strengthened the Polish Brethren. Quite a large proportion of the municipal council in the second half of the 16th century were people of faiths other than

Roman Catholic. The Cracow printers were also sympathizers with the Reformation. One of them was Maciej Wierzbięta, one of the most outstanding masters of the art of printing. Mikołaj Rej and Jan Kochanowski printed their poetry in his printing house, but mostly it concentrated on Calvinist literature. The development of humanism and the Reformation would have been impossible if the new subjects had not been helped by a powerful ally — print. The Cracow printing houses (Jan Haller, Florian Ungler, Hieronim Wietor, Marek and Marcin Szarffenberg, Maciej Wierzbięta, Łazarz Andrysowicz) made a big contribution to the raising of intellectual culture in Poland. It is worth pointing to the fact that in the first half of the 16th century 1,668 books were printed in Cracow.

In the second half of the 16th century, particularly towards the end of the century, the Reformation slowly became an élite phenomenon. The ranks at the believers in Lutheranism and Calvinism began to diminish. This was caused by a number of factors, very complicated as regards their origin. The Roman Catholic Church, after the Council of Trent (1545—63), made an internal reform "*in capite et in membris*". Discipline was made more strict in the internal life of the Church, higher standards were set and canonic visitations to dioceses were introduced. A lively publishing and propaganda campaign was started. The Jesuits rendered great services to the Church in the counter-Reformation campaign. The number of Jesuit collegiate churches began to increase in Poland, which had very well educated members of the clergy at their disposal. King Sigismund Augustus accepted the provisions of the Council of Trent and Poland entered the period of the Counter-Reformation. As distinguished from the western European countries, the Poles used persuasion rather than force to win over the people who had other faiths. Poland managed to avoid bloody religious wars that happened in France and Germany. At the same time, understanding was reached between the various religions by the Warsaw Confederation (1573) which ensured religious tolerance in the country. Moreover, an internal split, dogmatic disputes and mutual intolerance among the Protestants, particularly the Calvinists, repelled potential converts. However, we must note here that there were a number of acts of intolerance on the part of the Catholics, too; they were manifested solely in the form of religious disturbances, attacks on the meeting places of the Protestants and profanation of cemeteries.

Cracow also witnessed several tumults. The first of them broke out on 10 October 1574. It lasted three days and ended with the plundering of a Calvinist church. The Venetian Lucio Sacello, who was living in Cracow at the time, described the events as follows: "During the absence of the Cracow Voivode, who was visiting Proszowice, some dangerous disturbances broke out in Cracow, initiated by a religious dispute between several students and a certain dissenter, who when threatened with a beating took refuge in a nearby Protestant church, where a sermon was being delivered. The students forced to flee the church by the congregation assembled there, strengthened themselves, thanks to their colleagues who came to join them, and 400 of them prepared an attack on Bróg [the name of the church], which the dissenters had left, having been warned, leaving only the caretaker and the predicant. The students burst into the church and let the caretaker go free, but gave the minister a beating and then hung him up by his feet with head hanging down... The church was devastated in three days, a lot of things were looted and more than 30,000 florins were taken away. The Catholics themselves, amazed at the development of events, did, it is true, try to persuade the attackers to leave the church but there was no official among them who could make them return the things they had stolen."

The church was devastated again on 7 May 1587. This caused a lot of comments, but those who made the attack were not held responsible for what they had done. The disturbances on 23 May 1591 meant the end of the Protestant churches in Cracow. A tremendous religious tumult broke out in Cracow caused by several Scotsmen, who had killed a couple of artisans in a street fight. This was enough for the crowd, who plundered the stalls of the Scottish and French merchants. Then they set fire to the Calvinist church and devastated it. On the other hand, the Arian church built entirely of timber was taken to pieces, bit by bit. There were also outrages at the Evangelical cemetery. This was the final act in the development of the Reformation which then collapsed under the walls of Wawel Castle. From that time on there would only be a few

Cracovians who would profess the Lutheran or Calvinist faiths. The Protestant church was moved to the village of Aleksandrowice, near Cracow.

The capital, despite the catastrophe of the Protestant churches, played no mean part in the development of the Polish Reformation. The Cracow burghers made a large contribution to the history of the Reformation in Europe. The culture of the city was enriched by a new element, namely the religious innovations from beyond the Elbe and the Alps. For many years the Reformation was a factor inspiring the humanists of the capital. It introduced intellectual ferment and put new problems before the humanists, on which they had passionate discussions. In the social sense, the slogans of the Reformation aroused the poorer people living in the city. The relatively smooth transition to the Counter-Reformation campaign is to the credit of Polish culture. True, tumults were not a rare thing, but they were the sharpest form of fighting the dissenters. As far as this was possible, endeavours were made to use the Tolerance Bill of 1573.

THE ARTS OF THE GOLDEN AGE

The sixteenth century, when the two last kings of the Jagiellonian Dynasty reigned, is usually referred to as the Golden Age of Polish culture. Economic prosperity, the lively contacts Poland had with other countries, humanism and the Reformation, all this brought about the really stupendous development of the culture of the Jagiellonian monarchy in the first half of the 16th century. The artistic interests of Sigismund I and of his son Sigismund Augustus had a favourable effect on their sponsorship. Bishops, magnates and the wealthier burgher families followed the example set by these monarchs.

In Cracow, apart from royal patronage, the bishops also were very active in this respect. Bishop Piotr Tomicki (1523—35) employed artists at his court (Stanisław Samostrzelnik), collected books, embroideries, valuable carpets and eastern fabrics. He even kept his own artistic agent, Stanisław of Rzeczyca, in Rome. Among the outstanding patrons of the arts at the Bishopric in Cracow were Piotr Gamrat (1538—45), Samuel Maciejowski (1546—50), Andrzej Zebrzydowski (1551—60) and Filip Padniewski (1560—72). Padniewski and Bishop Piotr Myszkowski (1577—91) were sponsors of the outstanding poet Jan Kochanowski (d. 1584).

Artistic patronage was also practiced by the Cracow patriciate. The Boners supported German art. Jan Boner brought the painter Hans Suess of Kulmbach from distant Nuremberg. Seweryn Boner ordered bronze tomb plates from the Vischers. But in the lead were the numerous Italian artists, who worked to orders from the royal court and the burghers. They had family ties with Cracow. They came from beyond the Alps, settled at the foot of Wawel Hill, married burghers' daughters and stayed permanently. Italian art in Cracow underwent certain transformations, which were decisive for the Polish version of Renaissance art, which is a specific mixture of Italian influences combined with local traditions going back as far as the Middle Ages.

The sixteenth century was a period in which there was a development of the arts on an unprecedented scale. An important part was played in this respect by King Sigismund I. A pupil of the outstanding Italian humanist Filippo Buonaccorsi (Callimachus), while at the court of Ułászlo I in Buda he had personal contacts with a strong humanist milieu and Renaissance art; his stay in Hungary shaped his artistic interests. There also he witnessed strong royal patronage of the arts.

When in 1499 the west wing of the mediaeval castle on Wawel Hill was burnt down, Prince Sigismund encouraged his mother Elizabeth to have it rebuilt in Renaissance style. With this in mind he brought Master Francesco of Florence from Buda. It was not long before the Italian architect had rebuilt the west wing in Renaissance style (1502—05), decorating it with a fine oriel window. In the course of his work on the castle, Francesco designed a niche for a sepulchral monument to King John (I) Albert (d. 1501) who was laid to rest in the cathedral. This exquisite work of art was founded by the Queen Mother Elizabeth and Prince Sigismund. The tomb of John Albert is considered to be the first Renaissance work in Poland. Thus it was thanks to Sigismund that the first Renaissance work of art came to existence on Wawel Hill.

Shortly after ascending the throne (1507), Sigismund I began the complex reconstruction of the   56

Wawel Castle. He entrusted the building of the royal residence to Francesco of Florence, who designed a Renaissance palace and supervised the building personally in the years 1507—16. After the death of Francesco (1516) his work was continued by the outstanding Italian architect Bartolommeo Berrecci, of Pontassieve, near Florence. Among the stone-masons working on the building of the palace, there was Benedykt of Sandomierz — a great artistic individuality. In the designing of the palace, Francesco of Florence had based himself on contemporary Florentine designs. The fruit of these labours is a building of simple façades. The interior is divided into three storeys (two floors) and the ceilings are made of wooden, painted beams; in the representative chambers of the second floor (*piano nobile*) there are also wooden ceilings ornamented with coffers. The Deputies' Hall is one of the most singular in the palace: it has a coffered ceiling, with each coffer containing a carved head. They were carved by the sculptor Sebastian Tauerbach. Under the ceilings are mural paintings, done by Antoni of Wrocław and Hans Durer, the brother of Albrecht Dürer. The interior of the palace was heated by fireplaces, tile-covered stoves and by warm air pumped under the floors. All the chambers are full of light, which enters through the large windows.

The centre of the royal residence and also a very characteristic part of it, is the square arcaded courtyard, with its elegant galleries that enchant the spectator with their sheer beauty and rhythmic arrangement of the columns holding up the arcades. Only the second floor has no arcades, but slim columns which support the eaves of the steeply sloping roof. As a whole, the Wawel courtyard brings to mind the analogous solutions of the Florentine quattrocento. But there is no doubt that it has an originality of its own. Among the interesting interior decorations, mention should be made of the Gothic-cum-Renaissance portals, that are attributed to Benedykt of Sandomierz.

The architectural concept of the Wawel Castle was an inspiration for many Polish magnates' residences (Pieskowa Skała, Sucha, Żywiec, Baranów, Krasiczyn, etc.). The motif of the arcaded courtyard was also adopted by the burghers in building their houses. The Renaissance royal castle on Wawel Hill played an important role in the development of Polish architecture.

As well as thinking about a residence for his lifetime, King Sigismund I also thought about where he would be laid to rest and built a burial chapel by the cathedral. Sigismund's chapel is the most outstanding work of Renaissance art in Poland. In the middle of the last century, the German scholar August Essenwein called it "a pearl of Renaissance art on the other side of the Alps". The matter of its foundation and the course of the building has been thoroughly examined by scholars. In 1517 Master Bartolommeo Berrecci showed the king a model of the chapel. From Vilna King Sigismund wrote the following words to the burgrave of the royal castle Jan Boner: "An Italian came to see us with the model of a chapel which he is to build for us and which we liked; however, there was more than one thing we asked him to change according to our ideas, and we told him of these things. We also told him how much of the mausoleum was to be built of marble, and you will get to know more about this from him and the plan. Please see to it that enough marble to meet his needs is brought from Hungary for him for — as he said — Hungarian marble will be more suitable for such work than any other, and it will be more convenient to bring it from there. He also told us that he would need eight more helpers, who would sculpt the monuments, and when he gets them he would like to finish the chapel in three and a half years." This is the earliest mention of the foundation of Sigismund's chapel. As there was no longer any free space by the Cathedral, it was decided to pull down the Gothic chapel of the Assumption of the Blessed Virgin Mary which had been founded by Casimir the Great. The foundations of the Sigismund Chapel were laid in 1519, the walls were already built in 1520, and in 1526 the dome was raised. At the same time as the building was going on, red marble was brought from Hungary for the sculptures. The building slowly came to an end. The chapel was ceremoniously consecrated in 1533. In the following year a beautiful grille cast in the workshop of Hans Vischer, was brought from Nuremberg. Under the chapel a burial crypt was built to hold the tomb of Sigismund I. Thus this was the first modern royal mausoleum.

The Sigismund Chapel is square in plan and crowned with a dome. It repeats in its architectural concept all the features of the perfect type of building postulated by the Renaissance theory of art.

The interior is absolutely enchanting with its wealth of motifs and the ingenious, grotesque decoration that covers the walls of the chapel. There are masks, intertwined plant motifs, pictures showing the gambols of sea gods and goddesses, bunches of fruits, and the coats of arms of the Polish Kingdom and the Grand Duchy of Lithuania. The chapel is the work of the architect Berrecci and he was the designer of the general concept of interior decoration. The details were carried out by numerous co-workers. The author of the grotesques was probably Giovanni Cini of Siena. The figural sculptures in the royal chapel are the sepulchral monuments to Sigismund I and Sigismund Augustus and a slab representing Queen Anna Jagiellon (d. 1596), the sister of Sigismund Augustus, and in the niches there are statues of the saints: Florian, Wenceslas, Sigismund, John the Baptist, Peter and Paul. They are accompanied by tondi, placed slightly higher, with bas-reliefs of the evangelists and Solomon and David, all on medallions. All the sculptures, excluding, of course, the tombstones of Sigismund Augustus and Anna Jagiellon, were carved in the workshop of Berrecci, when the finishing touches were being put to the chapel. But they were probably not all finished by Berrecci himself, which is indicated by the differences in the artistic standard of these sculptures. It is known from the bills for the building of the chapel that Berrecci's workshop employed sculptors of Italian origin: Antonio da Fiesole, Guillamo of Florence, Nicolo Castiglione, Bernardino di Zanobi de Gianotis and Giovanni Cini of Siena. The outstanding sculptor Gian Maria Padovano collaborated with Berrecci. Until now the authorship of various sculptures and the monument to Sigismund I is not quite clear and still based solely on hypotheses.

The monuments to Sigismund Augustus and Anna Jagiellon are the work of the sculptor Santi Gucci, who worked in Poland in the second half of the 16th century.

As regards the equipment of the chapel attention should be drawn to the partly painted silver altar that was finished in 1538. It is wholly the work of well known artists from Nuremberg. The painted lateral panels were the work of Georg Pencz, and the magnificent bas-relief scenes in silver from the life of Mary are the work of the goldsmith Melchior Bayer. The designer of the silver plates was Peter Flötner. The famous musical College of Roratistes (1543) who enhanced service to God with their music and singing, is associated with the Sigismund Chapel.

The Sigismund Chapel is not only a magnificent work of art, but also a building which carries a complicated symbolical message, which together with its excellent artistic form creates a uniform whole. The symbolical meaning of a central-plan building is complemented by the religious thread, which is visible in the choice of the patron saints of Poland, the patron of the founder and the main apostles. St. John the Baptist was the patron of music, next to David, and the psalms of David were often heard inside the chapel. The medallion with the representation of Solomon was a reference to the person of the founder. King Sigismund was famous for his wisdom and like Solomon founded a temple for God. The concept of the chapel as a central-plan building reflects the perfection and harmony of the universe, as well as the perfection of divine nature. The dome, in this context, representing the cosmic order and heaven, was also a symbol of the canopy covering the altar and the tomb of Sigismund I. A canopy from ancient and early Christian times had been something distinguishing a person, emphasizing royalty and proclaiming a power given by God. It would be difficult to penetrate the enigmatic and complicated symbolism given to the chapel. There is no doubt that it was an exceptional work of art, which immortalized its founder and the artist who was responsible for its building. The Renaissance royal mausoleum aroused a sincere admiration in its contemporaries, as it was a pattern to be imitated. It also became a pattern to be followed in the building of many small chapels which were built in Poland in the 16th, 17th and 18th centuries next to cathedrals, parish churches, monastic churches and in Wawel Cathedral itself.

But royalty was not only interested in architecture. Sigismund I took care of the goldsmiths and the embroiderers, too. When furnishing the castle, he imported from foreign countries costly tapestries and fabrics with figural subjects, produced in Flanders. The most outstanding artists were sponsored by the king. In 1520, he founded a powerful bell, which bore his name "Sigismund". It was cast by a Cracow bell founder, Hans Behem, who came from Nuremberg. He also ordered a sepulchral monument to his brother, Cardinal Frederick (d. 1503) from the Vischers of Nuremberg. Sigismund I also ordered a Renaissance (1519—24) canopy to be made to cover the tomb of his grandfather, King Ladislaus Jagiełło, which was probably carved by Giovanni

Cini of Siena. Polish churches and the Cracow Cathedral owe to King Sigismund rich liturgical vestments and costly monstrances and reliquaries.

It is also worth noting that Sigismund I took an interest in the theatre, too. As early as 1511 there are mentions of performances given by Cracow students at the royal court. In 1516 the Latin play *Ulyssis prudentia in adversis* was acted, and six years later students presented Jakub Locher's *Iudicium Paradis* to the king and queen. It was the royal couple's idea that the outstanding Italian architect and art theoretician **Sebastiano Serlio** be brought to Poland. Unfortunately this wise plan was never carried out.

The successor to Sigismund I, King Sigismund Augustus, inherited his father's and mother's artistic interests. An ardent admirer of art, an enthusiastic collector of gems and jewellery, he was mainly interested in artistic crafts. He employed at his court the famous goldsmith Jacopo Caraglio, a contemporary of Benvenuto Cellini. The Wawel Castle owes its impressive collection of Arras tapestries which adorn the chambers of the castle to this very day, to King Sigismund Augustus. It is a particularly valuable collection (today 136 tapestries), something quite unique on a world scale. The artistic interests of the young king led to the fact that before the middle of the 16th century, the Wawel Castle received a magnificent set of Arras tapestries, woven in Brussels to the cartoons of Michael Coxie, called by his contemporaries the Flemish Raphael. The first news of the Arras tapestries purchased from Flanders is brought by a panegyric written on the occasion of King Sigismund Augustus' wedding to Catherine of Mantua, by the humanist Stanisław Orzechowski, and published in Cracow in 1553:

"After the banqueting and revelry and the games, the connubial couch was made ready deep inside the chamber (and it was brighter than usual) because of the magnificence of the tapestries, exceptionally beautiful and apparently not seen elsewhere in other royal chambers. On the tapestries there were Adam and Eve, our first parents and also the cause of our misfortunes, standing as though they were alive, painted by the weavers' art, both of them on both tapestries woven in gold thread. And because the figures of our first parents, apart from other details worth looking at, were distinguished for the unusual quality of the material and their artistry they are shown as Cebes wanted, so that the person looking at them not only knew the work of the outstanding artist who had done them, but also the personality of the noble monarch, which is best expressed by his liking for such things. On the first tapestry at the head of the connubial couch, we see a picture of the happiness of our first parents, in which as happy people they were not ashamed of being naked. And their nakedness had the effect on the persons looking at them to such an extent that the men smiled at Eve and the playful girls, who had been let in, smiled at Adam. For his uncovered nature showed him to be a real man and Eve to be a real woman." On the further pages of the panegyric Orzechowski described all the tapestries hanging in the bedroom of the royal pair. The collection of Sigismund Augustus consists of a series of figural tapestries: The Story of Adam and Eve, The Story of the Tower of Babel and The Flood. The series with The Story of Moses has not survived. The Arras tapestries depicting the fights of wild animals (*pugnae ferarum*) have a great deal of unique charm. The cartoons for them were by Willem Tons. The other tapestries with the coats of arms of the Polish Kingdom and the Grand Duchy of Lithuania, the king's initials and the ones with grotesque motifs followed the style of the artist from Flanders, Cornelis Floris. The fabrics, woven with golden thread, with a vast range of subdued and vivid colours, restrained by various shades of green, gave the chambers of the Wawel Castle warmth. They resembled the forests and woods, full of greenery, that Sigismund Augustus loved so well. The Wawel Arras tapestries were woven in the Brussels workshops of Jan Keempener, Willem Pannemacker, Jan van Tiegen and Peter van Aelst. At the time of the death of Sigismund Augustus, the royal collection of Arras tapestries numbered nearly 360. It is worth mentioning that the king left all the Arras tapestries to the Commonwealth in his will (1571), which is something new in the law practices of those days. Thus they became state property. The monarch was rarely in Cracow, but he left it a magnificent heritage, which today is regarded as a monument to his glory.

The family love for art was shared by Anna Jagiellon, the king's sister who continued the traditions begun by her father and brother. She paid particular attention to embroidery. At her court, costly liturgical robes were embroidered, which can be seen today in the Treasury of the

Wawel Cathedral. The binding of Queen Anna's prayer book, with motifs of eagles and her monogram (1582) embroidered in pearls is famous. It is kept in the Jagiellonian Library. She also founded the tomb of her husband Stephen Báthory (d. 1586), which was executed by Santi Gucci. According to tradition she spent a whole bag of gold ducats on the gilding of the dome of the Sigismund Chapel.

This royal sponsorship soon found people willing to follow in their footsteps among the clergy and the burghers. Berrecci worked for the outstanding humanist Piotr Tomicki (d. 1535), for whom he erected a Renaissance chapel by the Cathedral. Tomicki's tomb is attributed to Gian Maria Padovano, whose name is also associated with the tomb of Bishop Piotr Gamrat (d. 1545), which is a faithful copy of Tomicki's monument. Both of these works of art are excellent examples of Polish-Italian artistic connections.

Completely different in their artistic expression are the monuments to bishops Andrzej Zebrzydowski (d. 1560) and Filip Padniewski (d. 1572), which were done by the Polish sculptor Jan Michałowicz of Urzędów, who was soon to be called by those who came after him a second Praxiteles. This by-name is an eloquent testimony to the high estimation of his work which is outstanding in Polish Renaissance. Apart from being a sculptor he was also an architect. He reconstructed two cathedral chapels to serve as mausoleums for Zebrzydowski and Padniewski.

Sixteenth century Cracow was also a centre of musical culture which experienced a flourishing development under the patronage of the royal court. The last of the Jagiellons employed musicians and singers on a permanent basis. They played lutes, dulcimers, pipes, harps, organs, flutes and trumpets. The musicians played during banquets and court ceremonies. Of great importance for raising the standards of musical culture were the Roratistes. It was the duty of the Roratistes to perform *canto figurato* at dawn (*Rorates*) every day during Advent. The choir performed during many liturgical ceremonies in the Cathedral. The role of the Roratistes has been sometimes compared to that of the choirs of the Sistine Chapel. The Roratistes were active at Wawel until the second half of the 19th century. Sigismund Augustus sponsored many musicians, who formed a band consisting of several groups of musicians separately conducted. They performed sacral and lay music. Apart from the instrumentalists there were also outstanding soloists, virtuosi and composers. The instruments that went to make up a band then were the lute, theorbo, mandola, monochord, musical box, regal and dulcimer. But the favourite instrument was the lute about which Jan Kochanowski wrote the following words:

> The lute — leads the dances and scholarly songs
> The lute — a cooler of feverish minds:
> It softens the hearts of the gods of the underworld
> With its beautiful voice.

At the court of King Sigismund Augustus there was a famous virtuoso and composer, also an excellent lute player, Walenty Bekwark. Next to him there was another composer who also won fame in Europe with his compositions, namely Wacław of Szamotuły. Two motets of his, *In Te Domine speravi* and *Ego sum pastor bonus,* were published in Nuremberg. Another interesting composer, educated at the court of King Sigismund Augustus, was Mikołaj Gomółka, author of *Melodies for the Polish Psalter.* Nor should we forget about the third royal composer, Marcin Leopolita, about whom a biographer Szymon Starowolski wrote in the first half of the 17th century, that he had no equal in Europe as regards the beauty of his melodies. Among his compositions that were particularly highly estimated were the motets written cyclically for the church year. Tomasz Szadek and Cyprian Bazylik were also associated with the court of the last of the Jagiellons. The musical traditions of the court of the Jagiellons were continued later by the grandson of Sigismund the Old, Sigismund (III) Vasa, who took great care of the musicians, but their activity was in the period when the monarch and his family resided permanently in Warsaw.

To have a full picture of the artistic culture of Cracow, one cannot omit to mention the sponsorship of the patriciate and the works of art produced in the burgher milieu, taking as their models, of course, the works produced for the royal court. In the city use was made of the services of the artists working on Wawel Hill. Wealthy burghers — the Boners and the Kaufmanns — reconstructed one of the chapels in St. Mary's Church. To this very day people admire the beautiful gallery (1520) in the oratory built by Paul Kaufmann, which is a perfect copy of the gallery in the Sistine Chapel in the Vatican. The Boner family at their own expense transformed the chapel of St. John the Baptist in the parish church of St. Mary's. In the fourth decade of the 16th century, impressive bronze plates with representations of Seweryn Boner (d. 1549) and his wife Zofia née Betman (d. 1532) arrived there from Hans Vischer's workshop in Nuremberg. In the middle of the 16th century work started on the putting up of a tabernacle ordered by two vestrymen of the church, the goldsmith Andrzej Marstella and the chemist Jerzy Pipan, according to the last will of Tomasz Penczberger. This very elegant and outstanding work of art was designed by Master Gian Maria Padovano The treasury of St. Mary's Church began to fill up with costly chalices and reliquaries, a proof of the piety and care of the burghers for the principal church of Cracow.

Sixteenth century Cracow expanded very quickly. The population increased, too. The old mediaeval houses were reconstructed. And here we have a new and interesting architectural motif, called the parapet (a high belt of wall, topped by a comb-shaped decoration, which is above the crowning moulding, and hiding the roof). From the middle of the 16th century, many of the Cracow houses were crowned with parapets, and from the second half of the 16th century the parapet motif was accepted by Polish architecture, becoming one of its characteristic elements. The interiors of the burgher houses were richly decorated: they used painted wooden ceiling beams, mural paintings, inside columns between windows, etc.

The pride of the city was the Cloth Hall, in the centre of the Market Place. The old Gothic building of the Cloth Hall was burnt down in 1555. Soon afterwards the municipal authorities started the reconstruction of the building. It was made higher, the long main hall received a vaulted ceiling and the whole building was crowned with a parapet. Its characteristic feature are the gargoyles, designed by Santi Gucci. On the north and south sides, very picturesque Renaissance loggias were built on. It is thought they were designed by Gian Maria Padovano. From that time on the parapet of the Cloth Hall, together with the towers of St. Mary's Church, has been the main architectural feature of the Market Place. The reconstruction of the Cloth Hall was one of the biggest building undertakings of Renaissance Cracow (1556—59).

The picture of the art of Cracow in its "Golden Age" would be incomplete without mention of the hundreds of Renaissance epitaphs and sepulchral monuments in the churches (the tombs of the Montelupi and Cellari families in St. Mary's Church, beginning of 17th century), as well as the numerous old paintings which today can be seen in churches and museums.

In the first half of the 16th century, miniature painting developed to a peak never attained before. It was a real triumph. We should mention here the *Baltazar Behem's Codex* which gives a good idea of the daily life of the craftsmen, and the exceptional artistic value of Erazm Ciołek's *Pontifical* which describes the liturgical ceremonies conducted by the bishop. Both of these codices are among the most outstanding relics of the art of illumination at the time of the transition from Gothic to Renaissance art in Cracow. One of the most eminent of the artists in Cracow was Stanisław Samostrzelnik (d. 1541), who did beautiful miniatures, murals and easel paintings, still very much linked with the Gothic traditions. He was from Cracow and his whole life was linked with the monastery of the Cistercians at Mogiła, where in the end he settled as a monk. Bishop Piotr Tomicki was Samostrzelnik's patron. The artist did the murals in the Mogiła church and monastery, as well as a portrait of Bishop Tomicki, remarkable for its decorativeness, which hangs in the bishops' portrait gallery in the Franciscan monastery (the codices illuminated by Samostrzelnik are kept in the Chapter Library in Cracow, the Ambrosian Library in Milan and the Bodleian Library at Oxford).

At that time, there were many foreign artists staying in Cracow: Michael Lentz from Kitzingen (at the court of Bishop Jan Konarski), Hans Suess of Kulmbach (working for the Boners) and Hans Dürer. The painters belonging to guilds (150 in the 16th c.) worked next to the foreign painters. About 1520, a gallery of easel portraits of the bishops of Cracow was set up in the cloisters of the Franciscan monastery. The big portraits in this collection, of bishops Piotr Tomicki, Piotr Gamrat, Jan Latalski, Jan Chojeński, Filip Padniewski and Andrzej Zebrzydowski, were all painted in the 16th century. The person portrayed was framed by two columns or an arcade. The pictures are striking for the predominance of planes and their decorativeness.

At the end of the century, a man from Wrocław, Marcin Kober, appeared at the court of King Stephen Báthory, and painted a big portrait of the king. This work became a prototype for all Polish portraits for as long as two centuries. But Polish painting of the Renaissance never attained the heights achieved in the field of architecture and related sculpture. This was the result of its major dependence on Gothic traditions and smaller demand for pictures, but also due to the lack of great artistic individualities.

Summing up, it is worth stressing that what has remained till today of the heritage of Renaissance culture is the result of conscious artistic patronage. Cracow became the real Renaissance capital of the kingdom of the Jagiellons as a result of these activities.

In the second half of the 16th century, the Commonwealth had to face a serious problem of who was to ascend the throne. Until then the kings had been chosen from within the dynasty. The last of the Jagiellons did not have an heir. Sigismund Augustus died in Knyszyn in 1572. Before he died he ensured the unity of the state, by uniting the Polish Kingdom and Lithuania in a real union. In connection with these events it was necessary to hold an election for the new king as soon as possible. The principle of the election was what was then called free election, with the whole of the gentry taking part. In the period preceding the election foreign courts put forward candidates for the Polish throne, gaining votes in various ways. The place of the election was also decided upon: Warsaw. The gentry came to Warsaw for the election and the debates were chaired by the Primate, who in the interregnum fulfilled the function of regent. He too proclaimed the election of the new king. This way of electing was adopted then and remained till the 18th century. When the king was about to ascend the throne he had to vow that he would keep all the laws of the Commonwealth. The Henrician Articles determined the scope of the king's power and the rights of the Seym and the Senate. The successors to Sigismund Augustus relinquished the right of their sons to succeed them, and in the event of their breaking their vows, the gentry had the right to refuse to obey them. While in the rest of Europe absolute monarchies were being created, in Poland the king's power was being strongly limited.

The French prince Henry of Valois (1573—74) was elected as the successor to Sigismund Augustus. After only a few months of reigning as Polish king he learnt of the death of his brother Charles IX and escaped to France, where he reigned as Henry III till 1589. At the second election in 1576, Stephen Báthory, prince of Transylvania, was chosen. Anna Jagiellon was given to him as his bride. Stephen Báthory waged a long war with Tsar Ivan the Terrible and for this reason rarely came to Cracow. He was not interested in art. Thus the good times of the patronage of the Jagiellons were over for Wawel. These traditions were only kept up by Queen Anna Jagiellon, whose visits to Cracow became ever more rare. The centre of gravity of political and cultural life was now moved towards the centre of the state. The role of Warsaw began to grow gradually.

A new page in the history of Cracow was turned by Báthory's successor, Sigismund Vasa, the nephew of Queen Anna, but this will happen in another epoch.

CHAPTER IV · CRACOW IN THE AGE OF THE BAROQUE

THE DIFFICULT
17TH AND 18TH CENTURIES

How different from the earlier periods was the Baroque epoch in the culture and history of Cracow. The history of the city in the 17th and in the first half of the 18th century was a series of violent upheavals. The 17th century brought events which checked the development of the old capital of the Jagiellons. In 1586, Stephen Báthory died in distant Grodno. After ten years of the rule of this wise and ambitious king, the Commonwealth stood again on the threshold of a new election. There were two candidates competing for the crown of the Piasts and the Jagiellons: Archduke Maximilian of Habsburg and the Swedish Prince Sigismund Vasa, the grandson of King Sigismund I. The undecided gentry divided into two hostile camps. One camp was in favour of Maximilian, the other chose Sigismund Vasa. Fate decided that the election result would be determined under the walls of Cracow. For Cracow was the home of the Crown Treasury, and it was in Cracow that kings were crowned. The candidate who was able to take Cracow quickly was master of the situation. This was immediately understood by both candidates for the Polish throne. In the autumn of 1587, Archduke Maximilian brought his army to the gates of Cracow helped by those Poles who were in favour of his becoming king. From Sweden young Sigismund came with his army. Cracow was in favour of young Sigismund, who was a descendant of the Jagiellons. Continuity of the dynastic tradition played an important role here. Archduke Maximilian burnt the suburbs of Cracow and began to lay siege to the city. After several weeks he had to give up the siege. Sigismund Vasa mastered Cracow and on 27 December 1587 he was crowned in the Cathedral on Wawel Hill. He was the first ruler of the Vasa dynasty, which claimed the heritage of the Jagiellons through the female line and reigned for eighty years in Poland. After Sigismund III (1587—1632) his sons reigned in turn: Ladislaus IV (1632—48) and John Casimir (1648—68). These were stormy times in the history of the Commonwealth and Cracow. The siege of Cracow by the army of the archduke caused great damage to the suburbs, the people became poorer and there was a temporary economic standstill. Together with the changes in trade routes, the liquidation of the valuable mediaeval trade privileges and the stubbornly anti-burgher policy of the gentry — there was a definite regress in the economic life of Cracow.

Finally, and this should be emphasized, the royal residence was moved to Warsaw at the beginning of the 17th century. In 1609 Sigismund III and his court left the city to do battle with Russia. After the victory at Smolensk (1611), the king returned to Warsaw and lived at the castle. Cracow was still formally the capital of Poland, but the monarch's residence was from that time in Warsaw, where the central offices were also situated. The king was followed by the court and the magnates. The Cracovians lost numerous trade and artistic contacts. The only time Cracow came to life was at the news of a royal burial or a coronation. For it was only these events that demonstrated that Cracow was still a capital city, and the burial and coronation ceremonies left its inhabitants with unforgettable memories.

The moving of the royal residence to Warsaw had its good side too. From that time Cracow lived far away from great political events, the Seyms sessions and the Polish-Swedish wars, in which Sigismund III involved Poland. The Cracow bishop became the chief personality of Cracow. The life of the city revolved around the bishops, the cathedral, numerous churches and the Town Hall. In accordance with the spirit of the Counter-Reformation, new churches were built, the number of clergy multiplied and devotion flourished. New orders of monks and nuns (Jesuits, Cameldolites, the Descalced Carmelites, the Carmelite nuns, Reformati and Fate Bene

Brothers) arrived in Cracow. Holy relics and miraculous pictures became objects of cult and were worshipped by hundreds of the faithful. A considerable role in exciting this religious devotion was played by religious brotherhoods and the craftsmen's guilds. These corporations had their own chapels and their own patrons. Colourful processions and all kinds of church ceremonies supplied the people of the city with a multitude of impressions and experiences. The religious picture of Cracow was in accordance with the poem of Piotr Hiacynt Pruszcz (1650):

You are worthy to take pride in yourself, Cracow,

As a second Rome, so the proverb tells us.

The comparison with Rome was of course a big exaggeration, but it did give a certain picture of the life of the capital of Poland. The clergy owned the most property in Cracow. The estimated figures for the year 1667 are as follows: 55% property of the clergy, 16% property of the gentry and only 27% property of the burghers. Of course, this had a negative effect on the welfare of the city.

In 1642, Cracow had a population of 19,750. Taken together with the nearby towns and court settlements, it had a total population of nearly 25,000. In the second half of the 17th century, the demographic situation deteriorated and the population was reduced to 10,270 by the end of the 17th century. This was caused by terrible plagues (1652, 1662, 1677—80) which decimated the population. These plagues were an element that simply could not be controlled at that time. So we should not be surprised at the religious supplication: "Save us O Lord from the air, from hunger, fire and war."

In the middle of the 17th century a monstrous war reached Cracow. This time those standing under the walls of the city were Swedes. Sigismund III, from the Swedish dynasty of the Vasas, after the death of his father John III (d. 1589), had himself crowned King of Sweden, but a dozen or so years later parliament deprived him of the power to rule; as a Counter-Reformation Catholic, this monarch did not please the Protestant Swedes. But Sigismund III did not want to give up his hereditary claim to the Swedish throne, involving the Commonwealth in his dynastic plans. From 1601 there began a long series of wars with Sweden, which lasted — with intervals — until 1660. The battles were mostly fought in Livonia and Prussia, and it was only in the second half of the 17th century that they moved into Polish territory proper.

The young Swedish King Charles (X) Gustavus took advantage of the political and military weakening of the Commonwealth, as well as the lawless use by the Polish Vasas of the title of king of Sweden, for the conflict which had been growing over the years needed an immediate solution. Despite attempts to reconcile the two sides by peaceful mediation, an understanding could not be reached by them. In the summer of 1655, a powerful army of King Charles Gustavus attacked Poland from the north. The excellently armed Swedish army was mostly composed of German mercenary troops. On 31 July, Poznań fell, on 8 September Warsaw capitulated. A few days later the army of Charles Gustavus stood under the walls of Cracow. The suburbs were burnt down. After a fortnight's defence Cracow capitulated on 17 October. The commander of the Cracow forces, Stefan Czarniecki, then left the capital. Charles Gustavus took over Wawel Hill. This was the beginning of an almost two-year occupation of Cracow. The Swedes made the Cracovians pay high contributions which considerably weakened the city already damaged by the siege. At the same time the planned looting of works of art and books was started. During the period when they ruled, the Swedes plundered all the churches, took away many collections of books from both private homes and monasteries. The Wawel Cathedral suffered the most. For two years, the Swedish soldiers successively plundered that venerable church. They did not even spare the chapels and the Treasury. They profaned the relics and the tombs of church dignitaries. The losses Cracow sustained during the Swedish occupation are quite incalculable. In the summer of 1657, the Swedes left Cracow, forced by the Polish and imperial troops to capitulate, and on 4 September, King John Casimir and his wife Marie Louise entered the capital. An eye witness of the royal entry to Cracow, the writer Wespazjan Kochowski, gave this account of it: "When in regained Cracow there was more or less order, the King moved from his camp to the nearby village of Bronowice... At the end of the fourth day the King marched into Cracow without any ceremonious magnificence, as he did not want to give the municipal council any trouble and categorically forbade all kinds of pomp, only allowing a few of the most outstanding burghers to greet him privately. The sad look of the city could not be changed suddenly by the triumph: there were a lot of sick people lying in the streets; the corpses of those who had died or had been shot had not yet been removed. It was a painful sight to see the devastation of the city, which had flourished not so long ago: houses were in ruins, either razed to the ground or consumed by fire, the Market Place was fenced off with barricades and palisades and the alleys were full of filth and muck. The old religious rites had been almost ousted from the churches and if the city had not been recaptured, Lutheran practices would have been introduced there." According to the municipal records 47.9 per cent of the houses were destroyed in the years 1655—57. But it was not long before the city was leading a normal life again. Directly after the war was over, the Seym passed a resolution (1659) providing for the expansion of the fortifications of Cracow. The engineering work was directed by the architect Krzysztof Mieroszewski. New taxes were levied in connection with the starting of the work on the fortifications, which resulted in a decided protest by the townspeople. As a result the plan for the modern fortification of the city was never carried out, the only thing that was done was to surround some parts of the city with earthwork. The houses were gradually repaired, supported by the sloping buttresses so characteristic of today's Mikołajska, Floriańska, Szpitalna, Św. Krzyża and Sławkowska Streets. The damaged churches were also reconstructed. Cracow again began to throb with normal life, the only disturbance being the unpaid detachments of troops that the city had the duty to billet. Unfortunately the valuable books and works of art that the Swedes had taken away were gone for ever. True, articles IX and XII of the peace of Oliwa (1660) provided for the return to Poland of the plundered libraries and works of art, but they were to remain unrealized provisions of the peace. The war in the years 1655—57 was the most catastrophic as regards cultural losses. Apart from the plundering, the Swedes left damaged and destroyed towns, palaces, castles and churches. The size of the losses was horrifying and it took years and years to make them good.

John (III) Sobieski (1674—96) showed quite a lot of interest in the problems of Cracow, when he became king. It was in Cracow that he celebrated his first triumph over the Turkish troops in the Battle of Vienna (12 September 1683), making a triumphal entry into the city (23 December 1683) after the fashion of Roman emperors, and also admired a theatrical spectacle arranged in his honour by the councillors.

The repair of the tower of the Town Hall, which had been burnt down, was the only major architectural investment, made in Cracow during the reign of John III. The reconstruction of the spire and the clock took a number of years. John III presented Cracow with the timber for the construction and also recommended his architect, Piotr Beber.

After the death of John III, the gentry elected the Saxon Elector, of the Wettin dynasty, Frederick Augustus, who assumed the name of Augustus II when he became king of Poland (1697—1733). As a Saxon kurfürst he brought Poland into the long Great Northern War (1701—21) against Sweden, waged by Russia, Poland, Denmark and afterwards by Prussia too. From 1702, Poland became a territory where hostilities were taking place and also the scene of the mutual struggles of different political parties. Some of the gentry were in favour of the policy of Augustus II, others stood by the Swedish King Charles XII. The Swedes found themselves on Polish territory again as the allies of the anti-Saxon party. The unreliable dynastic policy of Augustus II was the reason for the Swedish invasion of Poland. On 19 July 1702, Charles XII beat the Saxons at Kliszów, and three weeks later took Cracow. Thus began another Swedish occupation (1702—09). The city was plundered this time by General Magnus Stenbock. Again the Cracovians were asked to pay a high contribution (60,000 thalers). To make matters worse, the Wawel Castle went up in flames on 15 September 1702, and news spread painfully over the whole country, for the symbol of Poland's statehood, a historic building, the residence of former kings, had gone up in flames. It was with difficulty that the Cathedral was saved from the fire. A contemporary account reads as follows: "The castle here was so badly ravaged by fire that the vaulting under two floors gave way and fell down. The fire at the castle lasted three days. All through Saturday and Sunday Sigismund's Bell was sounding constantly, to call people to pour water on the fire, but this did not happen early as the *summa* of the fire came on Saturday, that is, on the 16th *praesentis*. The other floor, *alias*, the lower one, which could not stand the burning rubble lying on it, broke away and when it fell, the people of various conditions who were there, priests, burghers *et alii* fell with it and were enveloped by a great flame and they were burnt until their very bones burnt too, others clung to iron gratings, but there was no way of saving them... The Cathedral was saved of course, but not without some damage in the place of the ciborium, because the chapels, going that way, had their metal roofs torn off, which laid the Cathedral open to damage from the flames, which were too near. People watched the Cathedral very carefully and poured water on it and they wanted to take the miraculous crucifix out of the Cathedral, they ran in to get it several times, but each time their efforts were of no avail." To add to this disaster, the country was also going through a civil war between King Stanislaus Leszczyński, who was allied with the Swedes, and those in favour of the dethroned Augustus II. Cracow, apart from the misfortunes of war, also experienced a violent hurricane (1703), which did a lot of damage to buildings, tearing off roofs and destroying the spire of the Clock Tower of the Wawel Cathedral. All this destruction was added to by the plague, which in the years 1707—09 caused the death of nearly half of Cracow's population. After the Swedes had left, Cracow was a pitiful sight. This famous centre of culture, municipal life, ruined by war and high contributions, did not have the essential financial means it needed. The drop in the value of money made it impossible to quickly rebuild economic life. As a result of the turmoil of war, the fairs were no longer held and trade was dying. The taxes from the burghers came in very irregularly. Cracow was forced to ask the Seym for help, but did not receive it. True, the Seym did recognize the claim of Cracow to compensation, but did not give any help. Only in the third decade of the 18th century was there political stabilization in the Polish Commonwealth.

In February 1733, Augustus II died in Warsaw. Poland was faced with another free election. Again there were two candidates for the monarchy; some of the gentry wanted Stanislaus Leszczyński, the son-in-law of the French King Louis XV, to be elected and others voted for Augustus III, Elector of Saxony. Augustus III was quicker getting to the capital and had himself crowned King of Poland on 17 January 1734. This was the last coronation the Cracovians were to witness. Despite the unfavourable political situation, the coronation of Augustus III was very well prepared by the Dresden court. Every detail of the scenario was worked out; suffice it to mention that the *Coronation Mass in B Minor* was written specially for that occasion by Johann Sebastian Bach.

In connection with the war of Polish succession (1735—38) and the Seven Years' War, Cracow experienced the harmful marching through of troops (Russian and Austrian), which also contributed to the downfall of the city. As a matter of fact, the example of Cracow is not the only one among contemporary Polish towns.

Against the background of the general torpor of those times, the positive personalities of Cracow's social and political life can be seen all the more clearly. Most of these personalities came from the clergy. Bishop Konstanty Felicjan Szaniawski (1720—32) contributed to the reconstruction of the burnt-out royal castle. His successor, Cardinal Jan Aleksander Lipski (1732—46), aimed at a reform of the Cracow Academy, although he did not manage to carry out his ambitious plans. His work was continued by Bishop Andrzej Stanisław Załuski (1746—58). He made efforts, among other things, to obtain the famous philosopher and mathematician Christian Wolff for the Academy. Załuski's reformatory efforts were frustrated by the stubborn resistance of the professors. It is worth mentioning here that, together with his brother Józef, Bishop of Kiev, Załuski created the first public library in Poland, which was opened in Warsaw in 1747. As Bishop of Cracow he showed himself to be an excellent manager and priest. He showed an interest in the reform of the social system of the state. He also wrote some very apt remarks concerning the plans for the reform of the state finances, the courts and the cities. In the middle of the century the voices calling for a reform of the social system and political power were gaining ever more support, and the programme of postulated reforms also included municipal problems. The year 1763, together with the death of Augustus III, brought some fundamental changes in Poland.

BAROQUE FOUNDATIONS
AND SPONSORSHIP OF ART

At the end of the 16th century, in Papal Rome, a new kind of art was born. Artists gave up harmony and operated with light and shade and were very fond of massive, monumental works. Picturesqueness, dynamics and theatricality were the main features of the new art which those who came later christened baroque. At present the notion of the Baroque epoch is being ever more frequently used, eliminating the term "baroque art". For art was quite different in the 17th century, and it was different again in the first half of the following century. Baroque was an epoch in which there were many different trends in art.

Despite her peripheral position in Europe, Poland was always strongly connected with artistic culture in Italy, particularly Rome. This accounts for the quick reception of baroque art, which left a unique trace in our culture. Baroque art put its stamp on the art of the whole Commonwealth of Two Nations. Picturesque baroque altar-pieces, figures full of dynamism, and monuments filled the interiors of churches. Impressive magnates' residences were built or reconstructed in this style. The theatricality and picturesqueness of baroque art suited the tastes of the local people to whom it was directed. If today we consider the Polish culture of past centuries, it must be irrefutably associated with the Baroque epoch.

The first baroque works "in the Roman spirit" were created in Cracow, which was still a centre of artistic life. The sponsorship of Sigismund III and the all-round cultural interests of his sons, Ladislaus IV and John Casimir, contributed a great deal to its development. Up to 1609 the royal court was in Cracow. Sigismund III not only sponsored artists, but also painted pictures and did some sculpting himself. The Primate Jan Lipski described the monarch's artistic interests as follows: "The king painted, engraved and also did some sculptures... silver and gold figures, church vessels decorated with pearls, gold chalices, candlesticks and lamps for the churches in Częstochowa and Loreto." These artistic tastes, not met with so far in the Commonwealth, were shortly to become the subject of scoffing and gibes on the part of the gentry. But the king did not let this worry him unduly. He kept artistic agents in Rome (Stanisław Reszka, Tomasz Treter and Andrzej Próchnicki), and brought many works of art from other countries. Nuncio Rangoni wrote that the king was collecting the pictures of Italian and Flemish masters. He was an all round patron of the arts.

The artistic patronage of the Vasa dynasty included architecture, sculpture, painting, goldsmithery, collecting works of art and looking after the theatre and music. One can safely risk saying that the Vasas brought Poland into the mainstream of European art. They were the patrons of the best artists, and their example was followed by magnate families. The art of the Vasas, particularly architecture, had a certain lineal quality, buildings were monumental, while at the same time ascetic in form, which distinguishes them from the exuberance and dynamism, characteristic of late baroque art. The patronage of Sigismund III was both the result of internal needs and the political tendencies of the epoch. For art added to the splendour of a ruler, becoming an instrument of politics and propaganda.

When, in 1595, the north wing of the royal castle on Wawel Hill was burnt down twice (Renaissance chambers went up in flames and the painted wooden beams and valuable furniture were lost), the king started rebuilding it at once. The architectural work was supervised by the court architect Giovanni Battista Trevano with the cooperation of Giovanni Petrini, Kasper Arconi and Ambroży Meazzi. The intensive work was done in the years 1602—03. And this is the time when the many marble portals decorated with the coat of arms of the Vasa dynasty (a Sheaf) and fireplaces, which were the work of the stonemason Meazzi, were made. And added to this there is the representative staircase (1599—1600) of the Roman type, designed by Trevano. The place of the Renaissance timber coffered ceilings was taken by plafonds filled with allegorical pictures. As early as 1599, Sigismund III had ordered pictures for the castle from the workshop of two Venetians, Antonio Aliense and Palma the Younger. Particular attention should be drawn to the Bird Chamber, decorated with pictures by the Italian master Tommaso Dolabella. It was unique for the sculpted birds hanging from the plafond, attracting the attention of the king's guests. Apart from the building done at the royal castle on Wawel Hill, Sigismund III also expanded the royal residence at Łobzów, near Cracow.

Royal patronage was also responsible for the building of the Cracow church of the Jesuits. They were brought to Poland in 1564 by Cardinal Stanisław Hozjusz. The Jesuits settled at Braniewo in Warmia. In 1579, Bishop Piotr Myszkowski entrusted them with the Gothic Church of St. Stephen in Cracow and the tiny Church of St. Matthew, situated next to it. Shortly afterwards, Sigismund III took on the duty of founder of a new church for the Jesuits, which was to develop a Catholic programme suited to the Jesuit doctrine. The building plans were worked out and then modified by designs sent from Rome, where the main church of the Jesuits — del Gesù — was being built. It is assumed that the author of the design sent to Poland was Giovanni de Rosis. In 1597, the building of the church was started. After many difficulties of a technical nature and the changes of architects (Joseph Britius, Gianmaria Bernardoni) the building was finally supervised by Giovanni Battista Trevano. He brought the building work to a successful conclusion. In 1619 the main work was already done. A dome was then placed on the church. In the years 1622—30, the façade was built. It is a modification of the façade of del Gesù. Certain jobs lasted until 1635. The stucco decoration of the interior was entrusted to the Italian artist Giovanni Falconi. The new church was dedicated to S. S. Peter and Paul. The Cracow church of the Jesuits meant the appearance in Poland of baroque art. The ground-plan, lay-out and composition, and the façade of the Cracow church followed the example of the mother-church, del Gesu. Trevano changed the proportions, the shape of the dome in relation to the Roman prototype, giving the building lightness. This was an outstanding work of art, worthy not only of royal Cracow, but of any capital city in Europe.

The building of the Jesuit church in Cracow became the inspiration for a great building movement in Poland. The façade of the Church of S. S. Peter and Paul was from that time the prototype for many of the sacral buildings put up in Poland. The founding of churches was an expression of more intensive religious life, after the Council of Trent.

Trevano also built a small church in Cracow for the Discalced Carmelite Nuns, which was called St. Martin's. He also worked to orders from the bishops. His works adorn the Cathedral on Wawel Hill, too. Bishop Piotr Tylicki founded three elegant gates and the wall surrounding the Cathedral. They were built in 1619. In the years 1626—29, Trevano built the altar of St. Stanislaus, which was founded by Bishop Marcin Szyszkowski. In this case the artist followed the example of the Roman canopied altars put up over the tombs of martyrs from the earliest Christian times. Trevano translated them into early Baroque style. As a result, in the middle of the Cathedral there rose an original altar, supported by four pillars which held up a gilded canopy. The materials used were gilded bronze and black marble. This combination of colours gave an excellent aesthetic effect. The same artist also made a sepulchral monument to Bishop Szyszkowski in black marble. It should be mentioned here that in Polish art, from the second decade of the 17th century, marble was frequently used. It was quarried at Dębnik, near Cracow. It was used to make tombstones, altars, epitaphs and also to cover whole walls of buildings. The Cracow churches were shortly to be filled with numerous works of art made of black marble, which gave dignity and stateliness to the church interiors.

Also in the first half of the 17th century, a hermitage and a church for the Cameldolite monks was built at Bielany, near Cracow. The hermitage of the Cameldolite monks owes its building to the powerful magnate Mikołaj Wolski. He also founded a magnificent church with a façade with two towers in the years 1610—30. It was designed by the Italian architect Andrea Spezza. Picturesquely situated among woods, the original composition of the whole complex and the excellent proportions, make it an exceptionally valuable relic of the times, an outstanding architectural monument.

This unrestricted building went on till the middle of the 17th century. Apart from great architectural creations, the old Gothic churches were also transformed and filled with baroque wooden altars (St. Catherine's Church, Corpus Christi) and sumptuous stalls (St. Mary's Church, Corpus Christi), and the walls were hung with huge pictures which hid the unfashionable mediaeval walls. Painting workshops did a lot of work for the Cracow churches. The painters belonged to guilds or were outside them (*partacze*), and there were also foreign artists, under the direct patronage of the king. Apart from compositions of a religious nature, there are also contemporary historical paintings. These paintings represented the historical events of the times, apotheoses of the military victories of Sigismund III and also family portraits. The artistic standard of the paintings of those times is very uneven. In composition graphic pattern books were used. The painters belonging to guilds generally preferred to accent the subject of the painting, artistic form being a secondary consideration.

The most individual painter of the first half of the 17th century was Tommaso Dolabella (d. 1650), who came from Belluno (Veneto province). He had a workshop in Cracow and many pupils, as well as a lot of imitators. Sigismund III, absorbed with models coming from Madrid, Prague and Vienna, wanted to make art an instrument for shaping the imagination of his subjects. Marcin Kober, who did the portrait of Stephen Báthory, was not the best of painters, and the Flemish painter Jacob Mertens, who was working in Cracow at that time, confined himself solely to religious paintings. So the king had to bring another artist to Cracow to satisfy his demands, as the local ones could not do this. As early as 1595, Sigismund III established contacts with the Venetian painter Antonio Aliense, a pupil of Veronese, who did several religious pictures for the king. The monarch was very pleased with the canvasses he received. He proposed the post of court painter to Antonio Aliense and invited him to Cracow. Aliense refused this offer, but warmly recommended his best pupil, Tommaso Dolabella, who arrived in Cracow towards the end of the 16th century. He settled permanently in Poland and married the daughter of the well known printer, Andrzej Piotrkowczyk. At the beginning he lived on Wawel Hill, where he had his workshop. In the first years of living in Poland he painted pictures destined for the renovated royal castle. Unfortunately these paintings have not survived. The subjects for his paintings were the political events of the first years of the reign of Sigismund III. For the Cathedral he painted scenes from the lives of St. Stanislaus and St. Adalbert, the patrons of the Polish Kingdom. These paintings have also been lost. He also painted large cycles of pictures for the Dominicans of Cracow. Only a few works of this artist have survived and they are badly damaged owing to numerous repaintings. However, Dolabella's influence on Polish art was enormous. At the court of the Vasas he was the only artistic individuality in the field of painting. Artists belonging to the guilds modelled their work on Dolabella's and the result was a specific kind of painting, which adorns many of the churches of the Cracow region. Pupils associated with the workshop of the Master (Astolfo Vagioli, Zachariasz Dzwonowski, Stanisław Wodka, Piotr Brygierski, Marcin Blechowski) repeated the patterns of the Venetian Master's canvasses.

The Swedish invasion caused a definite hiatus in the artistic culture of Cracow, interrupting the building and founding impetus. In the second half of the 17th century the following ruined churches were rebuilt: the church of the Franciscans (1673), the church of the Carmelites on the Sand (1679), the church of the Bernardines (1670—80), the Church of St. Agnes (1681), the Church of St. Nicholas (1682), the Church of St. Florian (1686). All the churches were rebuilt in baroque style, the original walls being preserved. The Church of the Discalced Carmelites, in Wesoła Street, which was started before the middle of the century, was completed (1683), and moreover in 1672 the building of the little church and a monastery for the Reformati was completed. At the end of the century an interesting church was built for the Visitation Sisters (1692—95, architect Jacopo Solari) with a Roman façade of the S. Domenico e Sisto type. It was founded by Bishop Jan Małachowski. A little later a modest church was built for the Capuchin Fathers.

In the Wawel Cathedral a new royal chapel of the Vasa dynasty was built (1664—76). Externally, it is almost an exact copy of the Sigismund Chapel. The interior is covered with black marble and on the walls are the epitaphs of the Vasas. The Vasa chapel, which was to be a dynastic mausoleum, was founded by John Casimir, the last of the family to ascend the throne of Poland. It glorified the dynasty that had passed away and strongly stressed its affinity with the Jagiellons.

In the second half of the 17th century, the painter Franciszek Lekszycki, a Cracow Bernardine, appeared upon the scene. He painted a series of picture for the Bernardine churches in Cracow and in Kalwaria Zebrzydowska telling the story of the Passion of Christ. While painting he used pictures of the works of the great Flemish painters Rubens and van Dyck.

The gallery of bishops' portraits in the monastery of the Franciscans also expanded. Distinguished among them is the portrait of Bishop Andrzej Trzebicki, which it is assumed was painted by Daniel Frecher in 1664 (recently it has however been attributed to the Gdańsk painter Daniel Schultz). Another painter of portraits was the Cracovian, Jan Trycjusz, author of the portrait of King John III. To end with, there is an interesting group of epitaphic paintings, painted on metal with a golden background. Eschatological subjects are represented by *The Dance of Death*, painted in the second half of the 17th century and kept by the Bernardines. It illustrates the doctrine of the church which was then being proclaimed: *Mors omnia aequat.*

Seventeenth century art was crowned by the erection of the University Church of St. Anne, which gave the city a splendid product of the work of architects, sculptors and painters. In 1689, the professors of the Cracow Academy decided to build a magnificent church in the place of the old Gothic one. The plans for the church were drawn up by the outstanding Dutch architect Tilman of Gameren, who had been working for years in Warsaw, building for the royal court and the magnates. The building and finishing work on St. Anne's Church lasted until 1703. It was a large church and was modelled on the Roman church of S. Andrea della Valle, with a façade with two towers and modern interior decoration. The stucco decoration of St. Anne's Church was done by Baldassare Fontana, from Chiasso in northern Italy. Educated in Rome, he made a thorough study of the work of Gian Lorenzo Bernini and transplanted his late baroque style onto Polish soil. Fontana gave the quiet architecture of St. Anne's the form of mature baroque, introducing into the sculptured decoration a lot of movement and fluent form. The stucco decoration done by Fontana made the interior very picturesque. Apart from St. Anne's Church, Fontana also decorated the interior of the Romanesque St. Andrew's Church and several halls in Cracow houses (Krzysztofory, 35 Market Place, 1 Szczepańska St., the Hipolita house of 3 St. Mary's Square). He did not stay long in Poland, but his work had a big influence on the local sculptors in the first half of the 18th century (Antoni Frączkiewicz). St. Anne's Church has an exceptionally beautiful painted decoration, which plays off Fontana's sculptures very well. The authors of the paintings were the Swede Carl Dankwart and the Italian painters Carlo Monti and Innocenti Monti. They represent a kind of painting that is not illusionistic yet, but three-dimensional, modelled on the painted decoration of the del Gesù Church in Rome.

The sculptured decoration in St. Anne's Church began another phase of Cracow's baroque art. This time, it will be art full of dynamism, sometimes expressive, representing fully the developed features of style in which the differences between architecture, sculpture and painting are erased and all three categories of art mutually permeate one another.

In the architecture of the 18th century well developed baroque can be seen in the works of the architects Kasper Bażanka (d. 1726) and Francesco Placidi (d. 1782). Bażanka was a student of the Roman Academia di S. Lucca. In his work he followed the example of the finished works of Francesso Borromini regarded as the father of mature baroque art. The Missionaries' church in Cracow is one of Bażanka's major works. The interior, adorned with mirrors, was modelled on the Three Kings Church in the Roman Collegio di Propaganda Fide (Borromini), and the façade also repeats the Roman design of the Church of S. Andrea al Quirinale (Bernini) and the Church del Gesù e Maria (Rainaldi). Thus the artist was repeating well known solutions used by the most famous Roman architects. Bażanka also designed the churches of the Piarists (1714—28) and the Carmelite Nuns in Wesoła St. It is also worth mentioning another beautiful work of his — the elegant spire of the Clock Tower (1715—16) of the Wawel Cathedral. It is one of the most beautiful spires in Poland.

The work of Placidi, a man of Roman origin, who had worked in Dresden on the building of the Katholische Hofkirche, was rather different. Placidi came to Cracow from the capital of Saxony in 1742 and spent most of his life there. His designs were in the spirit of late baroque. His architectural work adorns the Cathedral (the chapels of the Lipskis and Załuski, the altar of the Crucified Christ and monuments to Michael Korybut Wiśniowiecki and John III). The major buildings he designed and built in Cracow include the church of the Trinitarians (1752—58) with a picturesque façade, resembling the Roman and Austrian late baroque churches. He also built the flat façade of the Piarists' church (1759—61), which is a good urbanistic accent closing St. John's Street.

Apart from the above-mentioned buildings, one more historic church was built in the 18th century — the Paulite Fathers' Church on the Cliff (1733—51). It was the work of two architects, Antoni Müntzer from Brzeg in Silesia and Antonio Solari. Monumental steps lead up to the façade with two towers, creating an interesting architectural solution, rather similar to that applied in building the Church of St. John on the Rock, in Prague.

In reviewing the baroque architecture of Cracow, mention is due also to the polychromes covering the ceilings of the churches of the Piarists and Trinitarians. They are integrally connected with the architecture, constituting its spatial prolongation. Both paintings are of the illusionistic type and their origin can be sought in the paintings of the Roman painter Andrea del Pozzo (d. 1709). The author of the polychromes in the church of the Piarists was Franciszek Ekstein, and Józef Piltz did the painting in the Trinitarians' church. This type of polychrome imitating architecture was decidedly accepted in Polish art.

Among the 18th century painters of Cracow the best were: Szymon Czechowicz, a pupil of Carlo Maratti, and Tadeusz Kuntze, called Konicz, who was trained in Rome. The pictures painted by Czechowicz are in the Piarists' church, while those by Konicz are in the Missionaries' church and in the Cathedral. Father Jacek Łopacki sponsored a series of splendid pictures in St. Mary's Church, which were ordered from the outstanding painter Giovanni Battista Pittoni in Venice.

Late baroque forms can also be found among the works of wood-carvers. Attention should be drawn to Jerzy Hankis, who created the monumental main altar (1698—99) in the Carmelite Church on the Sand. The highest standards were attained by Antoni Frączkiewicz, who continued excellently the work initiated by Baldassare Fontana. His mobile and elegant carvings can be seen in St. Anne's Church (pulpit), in the Missionaries' church and in St. John's Church. Many more very good carvings are also attributed to this artist. Numerous, lavishly gilded carvings adorn the main and side altars of the church of the Bernardines; they were done in the years 1758—61 by the following wood-carvers: Jan Waga, Michał Dobek, Rojowski and Antoni Gegenpauer. These carvings have a markedly decorative character, the slim and mobile figures show a high artistic level. The stucco decoration in the Church of the Paulite Fathers has excellent form. Its authors were Jan and Wojciech Rojowski and Johann Georg Lehnert from Regensburg.

There is no doubt that the burgher architecture of the baroque period was much poorer. No palatial residences were built in Cracow. The few magnates' residences (the Zbaraskis' palace, Krzysztofory, the Spisz Palace) were densely surrounded by other buildings put up for municipal development. They were originally built by joining several houses together. They were distinguished from the burghers' houses by a larger courtyard or a magnificent representative portal. The houses of the burghers were constantly being reconstructed and their interiors transformed, and often buttresses were built to support them. Today these buttresses are features which give the city its special, unique charm, becoming a characteristic element of the scenery, although in the times when they were built it was the result of their owners becoming poorer. Another characteristic feature of the façades of Cracow houses are the arcaded, monumental portals leading into the entrance hall. The burghers willingly collected pictures and other works of art, which were kept inside the house and are often mentioned in inventories of property or wills. The artistic sponsorship of the Cracow burghers was mainly for sacral foundations. Valuable chalices, monstrances and chasubles were given to the church treasuries, and a lot of care was given to the churches. New chapels were built and existing chapels were transformed.

The church treasuries contain invaluable liturgical paraments. Most of them are the work of local goldsmiths and are equal as regards artistic standards to the works of German, Bohemian and Austrian goldsmiths. Of a very high class is the reliquary for the head of St. John Cantius (1695), the work of Jan Ceypler. An interesting example of the artistic contacts between Cracow and Gdańsk is the silver coffin of St. Stanislaus (1669—71), which was made by Peter van der Rennen, an inhabitant of Gdańsk, and is an exceptional example of the art of the goldsmith. The bronze lattices used to close the chapels in the Cathedral were also brought from Gdańsk (the Zadzik chapel and the Vasa chapel). The lattice (1673) closing the royal chapel of the Vasas came from the workshop of Michael Weinhold and is an interesting specimen of the art of casting. Royal coffins which can be seen in the crypts of the Cathedral were also ordered from Gdańsk craftsmen from the end of the 16th century. It was in Gdańsk that the coffins of Sigismund Augustus, Anna Jagiellon, Stephen Báthory, Sigismund III, and his wife Constance were made. On the other hand, the coffins of Ladislaus IV and his wife Cecilia Renata were made by a goldsmith from Toruń, Jan Christian Bierpfaff. It would be impossible to mention all the works of goldsmiths and the embroideries to be found in the treasuries of the Cracow churches. In spite of many disasters and plundering they are an eloquent testimony of the artistic culture of the former Polish capital.

In the epoch under review (17th and 18th centuries), various great spectaculars — pompous royal entries into cities, funerals and church processions — became a generally accepted practice. They were accompanied by careful preparation of decorations, designed by the best architects and painters. Gigantic *theatrum sacrum* and *theatrum profanum* were created. In the baroque period all kinds of lay and liturgical rites were, above all, spectaculars. In those years, Cracow witnessed ingresses of monarchs, great canonization processions, and triumphal festivities on the occasion of military victories.

The artistic culture of the baroque period left its stamp on the history of Cracow. In spite of the unfavourable political situation, the city quickly adopted its picturesque baroque attire, which despite the ravages of time, still arouses the admiration of the people of our times.

CHAPTER V · THE CITY IN THE ENLIGHTENMENT PERIOD

When Stanislaus Augustus Poniatowski ascended the Polish throne (1764—95) there began a period of great state reforms and changes in the way of thinking of the Polish people. These noble years ended in 1795 with a national catastrophe, when Poland was erased from the map of Europe and divided between three neighbouring powers: Russia, Austria and Prussia. Of course all these events weighed heavily on the history of Cracow in the years 1764—95.

The reforms started as early as 1764. During the debates of the Seym, a Treasury Commission was called into being, which was to look after the trade and financial affairs of the country. A Commission for Good City Rule (*Boni Ordinis*) was also called into being and its task was to put Warsaw's economic life in order. Another such commission was to be called into being in the future for Cracow. The Commission laid broad plans for the economic development of Little Poland and Cracow was to become an industrial centre for that region. It seemed that this economic reform, which had started so well, would soon embrace Cracow.

But the first years of the reign of Stanislaus Augustus brought the town considerable losses and destruction. This was because of the Confederacy of Bar (1768—72), one more fratricidal war destroying the southern part of the Commonwealth.

The Confederacy, set up in 1768 by the gentury, was against Russia and the king and was an act of protest against the growing political interference of Russia, and the direct cause was the arrest and deportation into Russia of four Polish senators who opposed the political conceptions of the Empress. A manifesto was proclaimed which spoke of the defence "of faith, freedom and violated rights". The Confederacy was set up at the small Podolian town of Bar and the Cracow region was on the side of the Confederates. The gentry of Little Poland was against the interference of Russia in Polish matters; moreover, among the senators who had been taken to Russia was the Cracow bishop Kajetan Sołtyk. Cracow's geographical situation made it easier for the Confederates to move about. The proximity of Austria, which was neutral in this conflict, provided the possibility of escapes abroad. So Cracow voivodship became the territorial base of the Confederates, and the most important battles were fought near Cracow, Lanckorona, Tyniec and Częstochowa. Cracow played an important role in the plans of the Confederates as a point of communication between Great Poland and the Subcarpathian region. On 20 June 1768 the gentry gathered in Cracow to set up a voivodship confederation and start war. During the four years of the Confederacy, the Russian army twice approached Cracow, destroying its neighbourhood and plundering the city.

In 1768 well armed and excellently trained Russian troops marched up to the walls of Cracow. The city was defended with unparalleled enthusiasm. All the Cracovians took part in the defence. The students of the Cracow Academy also made a big contribution. But the Russians would not give up the idea of taking Cracow. The city was stormed again and again. The suburbs were burnt to a cinder. Detachments under the command of General Apraksin captured Kazimierz. On the night of 16 and 17 August, the tsarist army started a general storm from the north, which ended with the taking of the Florian and Sławkowska Gates. In the face of this situation the town had to capitulate and the Russians entered Cracow. Then started the plundering of houses and a search for hidden Confederates. The Russian troops took up quarters in the burghers' houses. Several months later, the insurgents again took Cracow. The city passed from one side to the other. In 1772 the Confederates took Wawel by stratagem, but they were quickly forced to capitulate. But the Confederacy of Bar was gradually dying and in August 1772 Częstochowa, the last redoubt of the Confederates, capitulated. Cracow found itself again, as at the beginning of the 18th century, in the depths of decline. The city was devastated, in ruins, plundered and its suburbs had been burnt down, the population was decimated by war and illness and the economy was in regress. The situation of Cracow was sealed by a new political situation. On 5 August 1772, the three powers, Austria, Russia and Prussia, concluded a partitioning convention in St. Petersburg. The Commonwealth lost 1/3 of its territory to the partitioning powers. Austria took the southern part of Little Poland up to the River Vistula. Thus only the river divided Cracow from Austria. The salt mines at Wieliczka and Bochnia went to the Austrians. For nine months the emperor's troops were stationed in Cracow. The unity of the economy of the Cracow region was shattered and Cracow became a frontier town dependent on the customs policies of Austria, the Austrian authorities doing all they could to weaken it. Not long afterwards (1784), the town of Podgórze was built on the right bank of the Vistula and was to set up keen competition for Cracow. The Englishman, William Coxe, wrote of the depressing impression left by Cracow which he visited while travelling round Poland in 1778, saying that the big Market Place in the centre of the city was very spacious and was distinguished for the large number of well-built houses, once richly furnished and densely populated, but then either empty or sadly falling into ruin. Some of the streets were nice and wide, but almost every building carried clear traces of past glory and lost dignity. Only the churches seemed to have kept their original splendour. That unfortunate city was first ruined by the Swedes, when it was besieged and taken by King Charles XII in the first half of the century. But the misfortune that the city suffered from the plunderers from the North did much less damage than the later civil war, during which the city passed backwards and forwards between the Russians and the Confederates of Bar. One could still see traces of grape-shot, cannon-balls and rifle bullets on the walls of the houses. In other words, in Cracow one could see only the remains of its past splendour and it looked like a great capital in ruins; the number of demolished and tumbledown houses gave the impression that they had just been plundered and that the enemy had only left them a few days ago. The city was surrounded with a high wall built of bricks, strengthened with round and square bastions with the fantastic shapes of the old style of fortifications.

But in spite of the war destruction and the creation of a rival centre on the other bank of the Vistula, the Cracovians showed quite considerable economic initiative, and a strong desire to raise their city from its downfall. A number of attempts were made to bring a renewal in the economy, in the social system and in culture. They began by setting up manufactories (snuff, cloth, linen). At the same time a Commission for Good City Rule was at last set up for Cracow, which started to reform the social system of the city. The state of the city treasury and bills were controlled and an economic department and police force were organized. The effect of the activity of the Commission for Good City Rule was the modernization of the still mediaeval municipal organization.

Almost at the same time, the reform of the Cracow Academy was started. The organization of the reform was entrusted to young Hugo Kołłątaj, who in the spirit of the Enlightenment gave the university a new profile, more suited to contemporary needs. Kołłątaj found the Academy in a pitiful state. Instead of being engaged in science, the professors were making efforts to have John Cantius (d. 1473), a professor of theology, canonized. It was a very complicated problem and cost a million zlotys, a huge sum in those days. Attempts to reform the Academy, postulated by bishops Jan Aleksander Lipski and Andrzej Stanisław Załuski, met with sharp protests from the conservative professors. On the eve of Kołłątaj's arrival, the Cracow Academy was steeped in the scholastic method. It was a long way from the rational and empirical methods of the Enlightenment. This state of affairs had to be changed at once, particularly as educational reforms were then taking place all over Poland. They were being conducted by the Commission for National Education, called into being by a royal decree in 1773, which was the first Polish Ministry of Education. It was on behalf of the Commission for National Education that Hugo Kołłątaj started the work of transforming the Cracow Academy. After he had become acquainted with the current state of the Academy, Kołłątaj started its reform. Polish was selected as the lecturing language. The so-called moral sciences, composed of elements of ethics, economics and politics, were introduced. The mathematical and physical sciences were reformed, by directing them into empirical channels. Medicine and pharmaceutics were also reformed. A medical clinic was opened (1780), a botanical garden (1783), and an astronomical observatory (1787). This activity of Kołłątaj was supported by the following professors: Antoni Popławski, an economist, Jan Jaśkiewicz, a mineralogist, Feliks Radwański, a specialist in mechanics, and the medical doctors: Andrzej Badurski, Ignacy Rafał Czerwiakowski, and Wincenty and Jan Szaster. Kołłątaj brought the outstanding mathematician and physicist, Jan Śniadecki, from Vilna to Cracow. He also brought the painter Dominik Estreicher from Iglau in Moravia, to become the protoplast of a "dynasty" of Cracow professors. It was to him that Kołłątaj entrusted the department of painting and drawing. The above mentioned professors had a numerous following and created a centre of scientific and intellectual life again. They were certainly not scholars who just sat in their studies, but took an active part in the political life of the country. In 1783, the principles of the functioning of the reformed university were established and it was given a new name — the Main School of the Crown. The departments of theology, law, literature, philosophy and medicine were abolished and in their place two departments were formed: the physical and the moral departments. The first one concentrated on physics, mathematics and medicine, the second, on theology, law and literature. Undoubted priority went to the physical sciences (Jan Śniadecki), medicine (Andrzej Badurski) and the natural history (Jan Jaśkiewicz). Apart from this there was a group of scholars in Cracow engaged in studies of political economy and philosophy, representatives of the physiocratic school of those times. This trend, attributing the main role to agriculture, won a big triumph in the state, which was of agricultural structure. In Cracow it was represented by Antoni Popławski, Jan Śniadecki, Bonifacy Garycki and Józef Sołtykowicz. Hugo Kołłątaj also initiated geodetical measurements of Cracow (1785), which were carried out by Maciej Dębski and Kazimierz Szarkiewicz. This plan of Kołłątaj's initiated the first modern measurements of the city.

The balance of the cultural achievements of Cracow in the period we are reviewing should be estimated positively. The city played a dominating role in Poland as far as science was concerned. These achievements constituted a permanent value, which was developed in the following centuries.

It would be difficult to compare or contrast the artistic achievements of Cracow with the culture of Warsaw during the reign of Stanislaus Augustus, for every comparison would be unfavourable to Cracow. The second half of the 18th century — the epoch of classicism in art — did not bring any important works in Cracow. About 1780, two magnate residences were built for the Wodzicki family: the mansion at 20 Market Place and the mansion at 11 Św. Jana Street. Both of these buildings were the result of the reconstruction of earlier buildings. As far as architecture is concerned, they follow the style of Louis XVI. New university buildings were erected too: the Collegium Physicum (1791) and the Astronomical Observatory (1788), both in classical style. The former was built to a design by Feliks Radwański, and the latter to a design by the Warsaw architect Stanisław Zawadzki. Towards the end of the century, the Customs House at Stradom was built. The majority of neo-classical houses were built in the first three decades of the 19th century. They were designed by Szczepan Humbert, Feliks Radwański, Karol Kriszkier and Józef Lebrun. The above mentioned buildings cannot in any way be compared with what was built in Warsaw at that time, because Warsaw became the real artistic capital of Poland. Much of the artistic work done in Warsaw was thanks to the sponsorship of Stanislaus Augustus. The creative artists gathered there and the most outstanding architects of the classicist period were very active. At that time, Cracow became artistically provincial.

We cannot say much more about the Cracow sculptures either towards the end of the 18th century. Sculptors continued to produce baroque works, which filled the churches and decorated the façades of buildings. Classicist sculptures were limited to the modest ornamentation of the façades of a few palaces and houses. An outstanding work of the period is the monument to Bishop Kajetan Sołtyk, sculpted by Piotr Aigner in 1789. It links baroque and classicist elements. In the Enlightenment period a national theatre was opened in Cracow. The exact date of the opening of the theatre was found in an archival record dated 17 October 1781: "Permission is given to Mateusz Witkowski to stage a comedy on condition that he pays 50 Polish zł. per month." Witkowski gathered a company which was shortly to present a French comedy *The German Cobbler's Wife*. Mr. Witkowski's troupe adopted the name "Actors" and for several months they gave performances which were willingly attended by the Cracovians. In the spring of the following year (1782), Witkowski had to give up the function of "entrepreneur" of the first theatre in the history of Cracow, because of financial difficulties. But there were others to follow him. In 1787, Jacek Kluszewski took over the theatre and ran it almost continuously till 1830. The new "entrepreneur" gave the first performances in the Spisz Palace in the Market Place and from 1799 in the building in today's Szczepański Square. This building is still used as a theatre today. Unfortunately we cannot say much about the repertoire or the actors of that first Cracovian theatre. The only information we have is the very scarce archive material on the subject and the few play-bills that have survived. It would appear that the theatre presented light comedies, and melodramas, which were translations or adaptations of German or French originals. They also presented contemporary Polish authors: Franciszek Zabłocki, Julian Ursyn Niemcewicz and Wojciech Bogusławski. And these were the amusements of the theatre public in the last years of the Commonwealth of the Gentry.

Towards the end of the 18th century, Cracow experienced the short — but significant — period of the national insurrection led by Thaddeus Kosciuszko. The year 1788 was an exceptionally important one in the long process of social and state reforms. The efforts of the numerous reformers at last bore fruit. Demands were made to strengthen the state, to limit the freedom of the gentry, to increase the number of troops and to reform the obsolete structure of towns.

In the years 1788—92 the Four Year Seym debated in Warsaw and passed the postulated reforms. Municipal problems came to the fore in the debates. A decisive influence on the course of the Seym debates was exercised by the outbreak of the French Revolution and the destruction of the Bastille by the inhabitants of Paris. These facts encouraged the burghers of Warsaw and other towns, who submitted a petition to the king concerning municipal reforms (1789). After this events proceeded quickly. In March 1789, the towns had a lot of their former rights restored to them and this document became part of the Constitution of 3 May 1791. This was an exceedingly important act of law in Polish history, paving the way for new reforms in the state. In Cracow the administrative divisions were liquidated and the three towns of Cracow, Kazimierz and Kleparz and their numerous jurisdictions were united into one whole and treated as one organism.

The adoption of the Constitution caused a sharp reaction by Russia and in consequence the Polish-Russian war (1792) and the second partition of Poland (1793). This time only Russia and Prussia divided the territory between themselves. Austria did not take part in the partition convention. A Russian detachment marched into Cracow to "keep public order". The stationing of the troops in Cracow imposed upon the city the burden of maintaining foreign and hated soldiers.

Despite the political crisis caused by the partition, the spirit of the nation was not broken. A conspiracy campaign was quickly started by the people and soon embraced the whole country. Many patriots left Poland, emigrating mostly to Dresden. Warsaw and Dresden were the most important centres of the future anti-Russian conspiracy. Attention was also paid to Cracow and its importance in the national insurrection that was planned. According to these plans Cracow was to play an important role in the insurrection, the aim of which was to gain independent and sovereign existence. At the end of 1793, the conspirators met in Podgórze. On this occasion the conspirators acquainted themselves with the moods of the people. A major role was allotted to the professors of the university. Thaddeus Kosciuszko, hero of the American Revolution and the Polish-Russian war (1792), was chosen to lead the insurrection. This excellent soldier and commander had numerous contacts and in the French Republic had been given honorary citizenship. The conspirators chose Cracow as the place where the insurrection would start. They took advantage of the situation that arose on 22 March 1794, when the commander of the Russian Corps, Colonel Lykoshin, received an order to leave with the aim

76

of observing the movements of the detachments of General Madaliński, who had suddenly left Siedlce and was moving southwards. The Russian troops calmly marched out of Cracow. The city was left in the hands of Polish detachments, who were initiated into the plot. These favourable circumstances made possible the start of the insurrection.

Old Cracow came to life on 24 March 1794. From morning the bells from the Town Hall tower called all inhabitants to the Market Place. In the early morning Commander Thaddeus Kosciuszko listened to Mass in the Capuchin church, where he had his sword consecrated. About ten o'clock he went to the Market Place, where, in the presence of a large crowd, the Act of the National Insurrection was read and Kosciuszko took a vow on it. He was then proclaimed the "sole, the chief Commander of the whole armed insurrection". After he had made his vow, the Commander went to St. Mary's Church, where he repeated his vow that "he would use the powers given him for the good of the nation and the defence of the state frontiers and for regaining full sovereignty again". The insurrection authorities and the armed forces were then called into being. A flame of struggle for the independence of the country shot skywards in the former capital of Poland. Cracow was, for a short time, the seat of the supreme Insurrection authorities and the headquarters of Commander Kosciuszko. The Cracow region was an area of intensive insurrection activities. It was there that the army was organized, decisions were taken as to the form of taxes, and proclamations were made to the whole nation. At the same time volunteers for the insurrection army came to Cracow to enlist. The city looked like an army camp. Peasants from nearby villages came to enroll for the armed struggle. Craftsmen joined the municipal militia to keep order in the city. The inhabitants contributed money for the insurrection and women gave their jewellery and costly ornaments. The churches gave old liturgical vessels made of precious metals from their treasuries. It would be difficult to describe in full the patriotic atmosphere prevailing in Cracow during those memorable days.

The first clash between the Insurrection Army and the regular Russian Army took place on 4 April, near Racławice, situated a dozen or so kilometres to the north-east of Cracow. The Polish Insurrection forces, under the command of Thaddeus Kosciuszko, stood opposite the troops of General Tormasov. The Polish forces won the battle. In battle, the peasants from the villages near Cracow, armed only with primitive scythes, made themselves strongly felt. Commander Kosciuszko, to emphasize the heroic bravery of the peasants, put on a peasant's russet overcoat and gave the scythebearers the title: Regiment of the Cracow Grenadiers. Among the peasants, Wojciech Bartos and Stanisław Świstacki distinguished themselves particularly.

The victory won at Racławice did not, it is true, have any particular strategic importance, but its moral and political influence was enormous. It boosted the hopes of the nation in the success of the insurrection and also faith in Kosciuszko. It became the slogan for armed struggle in the rest of the country. Not long after, there were insurrections in Warsaw and Vilna. Cracow, on the other hand, lived constantly under the impression of the Racławice victory. Joy at the victory was everywhere. The Russian cannons that had been won were brought to the city. There was also a radicalization of the community, following the example of Jacobin France. From Vilna there was news of the hanging of traitors to the country. This led to the conviction that all disloyalty to the insurrection should be unconditionally fought against. All acts of treason were ruthlessly punished. But the radicalism of the Cracovians was a long way behind that of the Varsovians. They managed to do without death sentences. Only Father Maciej Dziewoński was sent to the block; he was accused of working for the Russians. A sign of the radicalism and acceptance of the Parisian models was the opening of political clubs. In Cracow, this campaign is associated with the arrival of Hugo Kołłątaj in the city. Thaddeus Kosciuszko was against political clubs and forbade opening any organizations of a political nature. Kosciuszko's orders led to the official closing down of the clubs. In spite of this, those who were in favour of the clubs met in wine cellars, where they had passionate discussions on current events. A few political manifestations were even organized, in which the Cracovians took part. At the same time, in spite of the almost general enthusiasm for the insurrection and the person of Kosciuszko, there were among the Cracovians, people who were secretly against the insurrection, for they were afraid of radical social changes. These people quickly left Cracow and went to the Austrian Podgórze district to wait there for the further development of events. Church dignitaries also left Cracow. The Cracow Chapter took refuge in Tyniec, which was then in Austrian territory.

Meanwhile, the situation of the insurrectionists had undergone a diametrical change. At the moment when the insurrection in Warsaw broke out (7 April 1794). Kosciuszko's army had left Cracow and was moving northwards. Cracow was isolated, without army backing and left to its own resources. The weight of the insurrection was moved to Warsaw. In Cracow the fortifications were strengthened and the walls of Wawel were expanded, creating bastion fortifications on the Vistula side. Ignacy Wieniawski had command of the militia and the small army garrison. Efforts were made to mobilize the largest possible number of men fit for defence in the event of a siege. According to written sources of the times they managed to mobilize 3,800 men. There was a lack of weapons, which was keenly felt by the soldiers. Russia and Prussia came out sharply against the insurrection. The insurrection in Poland, combined with the radicalization of the popular masses, created an exceptionally dangerous situation. The powers already had enough trouble with revolutionary France. Cracow was within reach of the Prussian forces stationed in Little Poland. The Russians sent their army to Warsaw, where the headquarters of the Insurrection was situated. On 6 June, Kosciuszko lost a battle at Szczekociny. The Polish forces were fighting against combined Russian-Prussian forces. The road to Cracow was open. In June, the Prussian forces came to the walls of Cracow and surrounded the city. At the news of the arrival of the Prussian forces, Wieniawski escaped to Podgórze, and the city capitulated. Only a handful of defenders managed to take refuge in Wawel and stubbornly defended it against the siege for several hours. On 14 June, the Prussians took the city. From Warsaw the only news was of the struggle of the insurrectionists and the siege of the capital. News came of the defeat near Maciejowice (10 October 1794) and the fact that Kosciuszko had been taken prisoner. People were horror-struck at the news of the slaughter of the inhabitants of the Praga district of Warsaw, where the Russian detachments commanded by Suvorov decimated them.

In the end, Kosciuszko's insurrection was suppressed. The last upsurge of men fighting for the independence of the Poland that was still free ended tragically. In October 1795, the three partitioning powers made the last partiton of Poland and King Stanislaus Augustus abdicated. The history of the Commonwealth of the Gentry came to an end. During the negotiations for the partition, Cracow became an object of sharp bargaining between Austria and Prussia. This was interrupted by Catherine II, who gave the city to Austria. After over 800 years of belonging to Poland, Cracow became part of Austria. At the end of September 1795, the Prussians plundered the Crown Treasury and took the Crown insignia of the Polish state. According to the account of Marcin Kratzer, this action was as follows:

"They started to open the iron door they had been shown, but all the efforts of the master were in vain, and General Ritz, getting impatient, had the idea of putting a gun to the door and blowing the lock open with a cannon-ball; but he was persuaded to abandon this intention by Mr. Kowalski, Margrave of the Castle, who told him that firing the gun might cause the ceiling to fall and bring untold damage to the whole castle. In the end they called the master locksmith of Cracow, Weiss, who, after looking at the door, said there was no other way than to remove the lower jamb, so that a man could squeeze through and open it from inside. And so it was, they chopped away the stone threshold and Weiss squeezed his way in and opened the cross-shaped bolts, after which all those who were not needed were sent away; the only persons to remain were Mr. Hoym, Mr. Lang, General Ritz and Margrave Kowalski. The cases they found there locked and sealed were put in the carriage of the Governor and taken to his residence." Shortly after this General Ritz wrote to King Frederick William II as follows: "I wish to humbly report that on 14 October 1795, the Polish state insignia were sent from here [that is, from Cracow] to Wrocław to Minister of State Count von Hoym." From Wrocław they were sent to Berlin, where they were shortly afterwards destroyed. Cracow was entering a new period of its history. It was the beginning of over a hundred years of slavery, an eventful period of upward flights and downfalls of the national spirit and of the city itself.

CHAPTER VI · THE DAYS OF SLAVERY
(1796—1918)

The picture of the Polish nation in the 19th century is a specific one. The Poles of those days were soldiers fighting for freedom, political emigrés, conspirators, wherever a struggle was going on for man's freedom. There were also loyalists to the partitioning powers, and good managers. But above all, they were rebellious martyrs fighting for the sacred rights of the Motherland. In this difficult period, numbering more than a hundred years, the only things that kept the Motherland alive were Catholic faith and the native language.

The cultural role of Cracow was now reduced to keeping the national consciousness of the Poles alive. Cracow had everything that was best in the history of Poland to date. It was the place where the Polish kings were laid to rest and the historic buildings of the city constituted living stones telling of the glorius past. Cracow was an historic city, which expressed in a specific way the identity of the Polish nation. These problems were present all through the 19th century and determined the exceptional role of Cracow in Polish culture.

UNDER AUSTRIAN RULE (1796—1809)

On 5 January 1796, after the Prussian troops had left, the Austrians marched in. This was the beginning of the first Austrian occupation of Cracow, which lasted till 1809. Then came years of doubt, but also of hope. On 27 August, the plenipotentiary of the emperor, Count Auersperg, received faithful homage in the name of the new ruler Francis II. On the territory of the third partition, the imperial province of West Galicia was set up with Cracow as its capital.

At the beginning of the 19th century, Cracow was described by Antonio Baldacci, who had been sent there from Vienna. We owe to him an exhaustive description of the former capital of Poland. The newly arrived foreigner was struck by the picturesqueness of Cracow, with its many church spires and the bastions of the defence walls. Wawel Hill proudly rose above the city with its royal castle and Cathedral. The walls of the city were badly damaged and threatened to collapse at any moment. The picture of destruction was completed by the stinking moats that were never cleaned. The nooks and crannies of the tumbledown bastions were inhabited by the poor and by criminals. It was found that the houses had not been maintained well and the beauty of the Market Place was marred by the crumbling Town Hall. A large number of other buildings, both lay and sacral, were in the same state. The students' hostels were badly damaged too. Stray dogs ran about in the streets and the poor lived in gateways and courtyards. The sanitary state of Cracow left much to be desired, although it did not differ much from the state of affairs in many large European cities, for example Paris.

The Austrians decided to put the city in order. They set up a special Office for Municipal Building. They did not bother with the restoration of ruins, all the tumbledown churches and houses were unconditionally pulled down. Many churches were pulled down in this way, for they had no owners and were falling into ruin (for instance, the Church of St. Stephen, and the Church of St. Matthew). Wawel was adapted for use as a military barracks. There also, two Gothic churches were pulled down, those of St. Michael and St. George. In the course of this campaign, which was continued during the first quarter of the 19th century, nearly twenty churches and the buildings connected with them were destroyed. In 1806, the Austrian Government issued a decree on the destruction of the tumbledown city walls for the repair of which there was not enough money; in the end the walls were pulled down between 1810 and 1814.

The Napoleonic wars that Austria was waging interrupted the destructive impetus of the municipal authorities for several years. However, the Office for Municipal Building drew up town plans for the further development of the city, which were carried out by the middle of the 19th century.

The partitioners reorganized the municipal authorities and the university. This meant the end of the mediaeval system of governing and the autonomy of the city. In 1801 a new municipal office was organized, which was subordinated to the state authorities and appointments were made by holding competitions. New sanitary rules were introduced: orders were issued for all refuse to be taken out of the city, the streets were equipped with lights and churchyard cemeteries were closed down. A municipal cemetery was laid out in Rakowice (1801) where to this very day Cracovians are laid to rest. In 1803, a change was made in the organization of the Main School of the Crown. Latin was restored as a lecturing language. It was not until 1805 that a fundamental reform was made, joining the Cracow Academy with the one in Lvov in one university. The best professors, led by Kołłątaj, left the university. Cracow lost its primacy in the field of learning, which had been so well-founded in the previous period. The germanization of the university took place gradually. Generally speaking it looked as though the city was threatened by a wave of Germans, both professors and officials, merchants and craftsmen. The last mentioned came to Cracow because they felt it would give them better economic conditions, which had prevailed in the city since its incorporation into Austria. The changed economic conditions led to a sudden immigration of Austrian merchants and craftsmen. This brought a lively development of production by craftsmen and workshops. Trade was also boosted. The number of inhabitants increased: in 1796 the city numbered 24,453 inhabitants, in 1808 it had a population of 27,278. The food industry developed (breweries, distilleries, confectionery) and services too (tailoring, shoemaking, furniture making). Capitalist forms of production appeared too; the first factories were organized from capital gained from trade. Transit and regional trade developed too, next to industry. The Germans who became permanent residents in Cracow were assimilated quickly and in time showed quite a lot of interest in the achievements of Polish culture. Cracow had always had a strong assimilation influence.

What, then, was the balance of the first years of partition in Cracow? Hugo Kołłątaj gave the answer to that question: "Cracow, when it came under foreign rule and ceased to be a frontier town, began to rise a little from its ruins and astute craftsmen and merchants began to return again. The government made endeavours to increase the income of the city and brought this municipality out of its debts to the extent that its income was enough to pay for all public needs and yet to have... considerable reserve funds in the treasury."

This short, favourable period in the history of Cracow was the result of a reorganization of the municipal authorities, stabilization of economic self-sufficiency and fiscal revenue. The favourable conditions which the invaders created were the result of the general trends in contemporary Austrian policy.

THE TIMES OF THE DUCHY OF WARSAW (1809—13)

The year 1795 did not obliterate the Polish nation's belief in the future rising of an independent Polish state. Shortly after the third partition, the territory held by the partitioning powers was covered with a dense network of numerous conspiracies. The community rose in sharp protest against the partitioners. As early as January 1796, there was an act of confederation formed in Cracow, which committed itself to rise in arms if the French nation called upon them to do so. The aim was, of course, an armed insurrection. Meanwhile from Italy there came the joyful news of the formation of Polish Legions to fight at the side of Napoleon. The commander of the Legions was Jan Henryk Dąbrowski. In Cracow the people learned about the successes of the emperor. They rejoiced at the defeat of Austria at Austerlitz (1805), the end of the Holy Roman Empire and the entry of the French troops into Poznań (1806). From the territory seized from the Prussian and Russian partitioners, Napoleon formed the Duchy of Warsaw in 1807, which constituted a substitute for a free Poland. The formation of the Duchy of Warsaw increased the activity of Austrian police in Cracow, aimed against the patriotic inhabitants. The political moods filled people with hope. This is how the fact of the formation of the Duchy of Warsaw was received in Poland: "Patriotic feelings and conversations began to be evident from 1806 and numerous young men managed to find various clever ways of getting through to the ranks of Napoleon's soldiers and every one of us took it for granted that it was only for this that we were growing up. The first patriotic songs were sung and political disputes were taken to the forest... The Duchy of Warsaw seemed to us a land of miracles, the promised land and both mild and stern ways of persuading us not to show these feelings were in vain."

Finally, in 1809, the desired war between Napoleon and the Emperor Francis I broke out. Cracow at last was to see Polish soldiers. On 15 July, detachments commanded by Prince Józef Poniatowski marched into the city. The Cracovians gave their fellow countrymen an enthusiastic welcome. The daily *Gazeta Krakowska* wrote as follows: "Yesterday, after 15 years of not having seen them and 13 years of German rule, Cracow at last saw Polish soldiers... At six o'clock in the morning, the Polish soldiers under the command of Prince Józef Poniatowski entered the city by Florian's Gate to the joyful shouts of the inhabitants... In the evening the whole city, by the citizens' own will, was decorated with allegories and suitable verses on illuminated banners." This was in fact the joining of Cracow to the Duchy of Warsaw. The Peace of Schönbrunn (1809) incorporated into the Duchy all the territory taken by the Austrians in the third partition. Cracow and **Podgórze** became a fragment of the independent motherland. A department was formed of Cracow and the surrounding region and Count Stanisław Wodzicki was appointed its head. At the end of the year, Kołłątaj came to Cracow for the second time to deal with university problems. Cracow was entering a new stage of its history.

As far as the economy was concerned, Cracow was joined to the tariff region of the Duchy of Warsaw (1810). Through the efforts on the part of merchants Cracow and Podgórze were made a free market city. This privilege created excellent conditions for future economic development. But the Duchy of Warsaw did not last long enough for the advantages of this to be fully felt. In 1810, a sumptuous welcome was given to the ducal pair Frederick Augustus and Beatrix. There was general joy at the regaining of independence. The sight of the Polish uniform gave great satisfaction to the Cracovians. But this idyllic time was slowly coming to an end.

The year 1812 was under the sign of Mars. The Franco-Russian war broke out. Napoleon marched with his army towards Moscow. The army of the Duchy of Warsaw took part in that campaign. A hospital for Napoleon's army was located in Cracow for the time of war. The emperor's defeat and his retreat from Moscow followed. After Napoleon's defeat, part of the Duchy of Warsaw was taken by the Russian army at the beginning of 1813; in February and March the civil and military authorities of the Duchy came to Cracow, which was the only place in the country where the government, the army and political thought could take refuge. Aristocratic families, who had fled in panic from the Russians, were swarming under Wawel Hill. Here also the Polish regiments under the command of Prince Józef Poniatowski were stationed. New volunteers joined the army and a detachment of "Krakusy" was formed. Cracow, despite the war, was throbbing with life. Balls and social gatherings were on the agenda all the time. However, the seeming gaiety and merrymaking hid anxious thoughts about the future. At the beginning of May (1813) Prince Józef Poniatowski left Cracow with his army, heading for Saxony. When the allied powers set up an anti-Napoleonic coalition, the Polish detachments remained loyal to the emperor. On 15 May Russian troops marched into Cracow under the command of General Sacken. The Russians occupied Cracow for two years. To make matters worse, in August the River Vistula overflowed causing floods which inundated Kazimierz, Stradom and Podgórze, and swept away bridges. The losses were enormous. *Gazeta Krakowska* (No. 69, 29 August 1813) gave the following report:

"On 26 August the level of the Vistula near Cracow rose so high and so quickly, probably due to the heavy rain in the mountains, that even the oldest people living in Cracow could not remember a similar flood, for it was worse than the floods of 1774. In a moment the waters flooded both banks and rose so high that even on the highest points of the banks it came up to the roofs... The suburbs from the Vistula up to the Vistula Gate, as well as the suburbs of Stradom, Kazimierz, Podgórze, etc. were flooded and damaged."

Meanwhile from Saxony came the menacing echoes of war. On 16 October, the fierce Battle of the Nations was waged at Leipzig, during which Prince Józef Poniatowski died and from that time on he has been a legendary national hero. News of the tragic death of the Polish commander filled Cracow with mourning. The little spark of courage and the hopes placed in the Prince had gone. With an increasing frequency the Cracovians were asking themselves: what now? They were asking themselves the same question when in 1814 they greeted the Russian emperor Alexander I. True, the tsar did not want to accept the municipal keys, saying he was a friend, but he was in fact the representative of one of the partitioning powers.

The problem of Cracow assumed international importance. It began to arouse the anxiety and interest of diplomats. The Napoleonic era had come to an end and Europe had to face problems of a new social and political order. What would be the future fate of Cracow?

THE REPUBLIC OF CRACOW (1815—46)

The new order in Europe was dealt with by an international conference. Representatives of the victorious anti-Napoleonic coalition gathered on 3 November 1814, in Vienna. The Congress of Vienna was guided by two fundamental principles, restoration and legitimism. The Polish problem was one of the most thorny ones. Russia, Prussia and Austria were all fighting for the division of the Duchy of Warsaw. Cracow and the surrounding region was a bone of contention between the powers. Neither Prussia nor Austria wanted Cracow to go to Russia. Tsar Alexander proposed making Cracow and its immediate vicinity a neutral territory — a free city. In Tsar Alexander's concept Podgórze was to be included in the area of the city. This complicated problem was solved by the political situation that arose when Napoleon suddenly left Elba and in April (1815) reached French soil, beginning the famous Hundred Days. This caused a lot of commotion among the participants in the debates in Vienna, aroused a spirit of compromise and accelerated the conclusion of suitable treaties. The fruit of all this agitation and the conciliatory atmosphere it brought, was the regulation of the problem of Cracow.

On 3 May 1815, Austria, Prussia and Russia concluded the final understanding concerning Cracow. The "free, independent and strictly neutral city of Cracow and its region" was called into being and was to remain under the care of the three powers. This agreement came into force after it had been introduced to the final document of the Congress of Vienna, which was signed on 9 June 1815. A miniature country, popularly known as the Republic of Cracow, came into being. It covered an area of barely 1,150 sq. kilometres and had a population of 87,986 in 1815. The treaty guaranteed the Cracovians freedom of trade, the possibility of importing goods without paying tariffs, freedom of activity for the university, and the abolition of the right to asylum for political agents. Cracow had diplomatic relations with other European countries only through the mediation of the powers who exercised supervision over the city.

Internal relations and the organization of the authorities were regulated by the constitution given the city in 1818, which was modelled on the provisions of the final document of the Congress of Vienna of 3 May 1815. The Constitution guaranteed freedom and equality in the eyes of the law, freedom to profess the religion of one's choice and recognition of the Roman Catholic faith as the prevalent one. It also dealt with the question of the peasants. They received personal freedom and were able to avail themselves of political rights collectively. The peasants were promised an agrarian reform, which was to be carried out in state lands by the Peasant Commission. The Constitution also guaranteed the inviolability of private property and freedom of publication.

The legislative body of the Republic was the Chamber of Representatives (41 persons), and the Seym met once a year. The executive body was the Governing Senate, which consisted of a chairman and 12 senators, elected by the Seym, the university and the chapter. Half of the senators were elected for life and half were changed every year. But representatives of the three partitioning powers kept interfering in the internal matters of the Free City. They were constantly afraid of revolutionary plots and student and youth movements. Particularly after the fall of the November Insurrection (1831) the three powers sharpened their control of the Free City.

In the Republic of Cracow the rapid development of trade made it a time of the quick accumulation of wealth by the inhabitants of the city. Merchants and craftsmen lived through a period of prosperity. Trade contacts were established with almost the whole of Europe, and a railway was built and opened in 1847. In the social field, the period of the Free City was marked for constant clashes between the gentry and the burghers. In a city which had strong traditions of self-government the gentry had the leading place, led by the Chairman of the Senate, Stanisław Wodzicki. The gentry accounted for a decided majority in the Senate. The aristocracy and the gentry formed an isolated social group, who kept to themselves. During the debates of the Chamber of Representatives there were constant clashes of opinion.

The Jagiellonian University, which on the basis of the statute of 1818 had full autonomy, played a very important role. It was then that the Academy finally adopted the name "Jagiellonian University" which has lasted till today. The university was the superior authority for all schools in the Free City. The professors represented the ideas of liberalism. The students came out sharply against the conservative line of policy which Wodzicki represented, and also fought with the police. In 1820, it even came to student demonstrations against an inspector of the police A. Kostecki. Those responsible for the disturbances were sent away from Cracow. The university had its autonomy withdrawn and a new statute, which limited the rights of the university, was imposed upon it.

Of momentous importance in the history of the Free State of Cracow was the stormy year 1830. In the first days of December news came of the outbreak of a national insurrection against Russia. (Warsaw, after the Congress of Vienna, was the capital of the Polish Kingdom, which was linked by a personal union with Russia and fully subordinated to the tsar). In the history of Poland this is called the November Insurrection. In Warsaw, the National Government was formed. Patriotic fever swept through Cracow. People were in favour of reaching for arms. Detachments of student youth went to assist fighting Warsaw. But the policy of the Governing Senate kept a neutral position which was consistently observed by Stanisław Wodzicki. On 16 January 1831, Wodzicki was arrested by young people, and resigned from his post under the pressure of public opinion and left Cracow. The fate of the city in these heated days was closely linked with the further development of events in Warsaw. In the meantime the Russians had started a fierce suppression of the Insurrection and the tsar's army scored one success after another. In September (1831) the Russian troops marched into Cracow and began a preventive occupation of the city. The Russians stayed in Cracow till 5 October, when Austria issued a violent protest against the annexation of Cracow by Russia. In 1831, the November Insurrection was on its deathbed. The first upsurge of the Polish nation for independence had fatal results. The repressions the Polish population suffered under Russian rule were terrible. Hundreds of insurgents were forced to emigrate. France and England gave refuge to these emigrés.

The Insurrection had an unfortunate aftermath for Cracow. The independence of the Free City was limited. In 1833 a new Constitution was introduced, which forbade Cracovians to interfere in the Polish problems of the other partitioned parts of Poland. The power of the reactionary Senate was strengthened, the prerogatives of the Seym which from that time only met every three years were reduced. Debatable questions between the Seym and the Senate were decided by the resident representatives of the powers that supervised the city.

The structure of the university was also changed and based on Austrian models. The rector was deprived of all powers, which were given to a government commissioner. The faculties were from that time staffed by winners of competitions, the results of which were confirmed by the representatives of the three partitioning powers. Some of the faculties of the university were liquidated and new programmes of studies were introduced.

A secret understanding among the partitioning powers (1833) envisaged the occupation of Cracow in the event of a revolution breaking out in the city. But despite these sharpened political measures and the limitation of freedom, liberal trends gained a place for themselves in the city. The Republic of Cracow became the mainstay of liberal and revolutionary movements, a centre of conspiracy. The fall of the November Insurrection was not under any circumstances the equivalent of the fall of national liberation thought. The emigrés conducted heated discussions and disputes about the Insurrection and the reasons for its fall. In Paris (1832) a Society for Democratic Poland was formed, which played a major role in the development of the ideology of emigrés and of Poland. Almost at the same time various independence organizations came into being. A large part of them was associated with Free Masonry. All the organizations which came into being abroad, sent their emissaries to Poland. Conspirators appeared all over Poland, but the largest number were in Galicia. Cracow played an important role then as a centre of conspiracy. Political activity in the Free City did, however, make the police more vigilant. In 1838, mass arrests were made, mainly among the young people. The Cracow prisons were swarming with prisoners. In spite of these repressions, this political activity did not stop. In the 1840's, Ludwik Mierosławski came to the fore among the conspirators, as an excellent organizer of an extensive conspiratorial network. Edward Dembowski, a spokesman of the left-wing of the democratic movement, was in permanent contact with him. The preparations for the insurrection were already made. Advantage was also taken of the inflamed moods of the rural population, which was demanding the abolition of serfdom and the handing over of land to the peasants. Liaison between the conspirators of the three partitioned parts of Poland was maintained by Edward Dembowski. Gradually he grew into the actual leader of the future insurrection, cultivating the concept of a people's war against both feudal oppression and the partitioners. The authorities of the Society for Democratic Poland named Mierosławski as the commander of the insurrection. According to the plans, it was supposed to embrace all the partitioned parts of Poland, but it was aimed, above all, at Russia.

The outbreak of the insurrection was preceded by a conference at which a secret National Government was elected. Jan Tyssowski represented Galicia in the new authorities, and Cracow was represented by Ludwik Gorzkowski. The date when the fighting was to begin was planned for the night of the 20th of February. But, in spite of the strict secrecy, information of the armed rebellion got through to the partitioning power. Then came mass arrests and on 18 February Austrian troops marched into Cracow. But on the night of the 20th of February — as planned — there was fighting in Cracow. The shooting lasted all night. The first men were killed and wounded. The Austrian commander, General Collin, withdrew to Podgórze with his men. The National Government appeared quickly and its first action was to issue a "Manifesto to the Polish Nation", which proclaimed equality for all citizens, the abolition of feudal privileges, the abolition of serfdom and rents and giving the peasants land which would be their own. But there was shortly to be strife within the government. Jan Tyssowski proclaimed himself to be the dictator of the insurrection; meanwhile, on 24 February, Edward Dembowski appeared in the city, and the insurrectionary left-wing felt stronger. At the same time, menacing news came of the fierce rebellion of the peasants in Galicia, who had plundered and burnt the manors of the gentry and murdered people. The rebellion of the peasants against the gentry was incited by the Austrian authorities. Information also came that the Austrians were gathering troops and encircling Cracow. On 27 February, Colonel Benedek took Wieliczka and the emperor's troops stood outside Cracow. Dembowski still tried to agitate the peasants to rise in arms. He himself headed a procession that moved from Cracow in the direction of Podgórze, but after they had left the city the Austrians fired shots at the procession and Dembowski was mortally wounded. The short-lived insurrection had ended. Detachments of insurrectionists, numbering about 500 men, withdrew to the west and crossed the frontier into the Prussian zone, where they immediately gave up their arms. The Austrians again marched into Cracow. Then began a period of repressions and many people were arrested. The Cracow revolution in 1846 put an end to the Republic of Cracow and on 6 November of the same year, Ferdinand, the Austrian emperor, incorporated Cracow into the Habsburg monarchy.

Against the background of these political events, the culture of the Free City flourished. In the liberal Republic of Cracow there were favourable conditions for the development of national life. For dismembered Poland, Cracow was a source of national consciousness and identity, a lasting symbol of independence. Of course, the leading place was held by Wawel Hill, with its cathedral and royal tombs. The tomb, in the period of the Romanticism, became not only a symbol of transition, but also had patriotic meaning, arousing people to action. Adam Mickiewicz called Cracow "the Rome of the Slavs". It had historic monuments which, in the years of bondage, taught people the history of their motherland. Cracow was a volume of national history, the sanctuary of Poland. With veneration people admired the works of art gathered here, feeling deeply the loss of independence, but believing in the unfathomable verdicts of Providence. The poet Wincenty Pol gave an eloquent picture of the new role of Cracow in a description of his arrival in the city (1834): "Cracow! Cracow! What that one word means to a Pole. Arriving in Cracow, anyone who was not a Pole before, becomes one." Perhaps there is a pinch of romantic exaggeration, a little pathos, in this declaration, but it was the honest truth, for Cracow was identified with being Polish, it was a symbol of the Polish nation and its culture.

The former royal metropolis now became the place where national heroes were laid to rest. In 1817 the ashes of Prince Józef Poniatowski were buried in the cathedral, and the following year brought the funeral of Thaddeus Kosciuszko. Both of these ceremonies were given an appropriate patriotic setting and news of these events spread all over Poland. Shortly afterwards the nation raised a symbolical mound for Kościuszko, modelling it on the prehistoric mounds to Krakus and Wanda. The Mound to Kościuszko, completed in 1823, became part of the Cracow panorama. Inside the mound, an urn with earth from the battlefields where the Commander fought, was placed. National heroes became figures of cult and for many years provided models of behaviour for their fellow countrymen. These patriotic manifestations aroused the national spirit, spread Polish traditions, enabling the people to live through the difficult years of bondage. These things favoured the development of culture and they also gave Cracow a very important social function — it became a sanctuary of Polishness and national life. These romantic tendencies were to influence the history of the city for the whole of the 19th century and continued to do so until the outbreak of the First World War.

An exuberant scientific life also developed apart from the Jagiellonian University. In 1816, the Cracow Learned Society, gathering together outstanding scholars and lovers of science, and connected with the university, was founded. It inaugurated its activity in 1816 and during the following sixty years played an important part in Polish science. The aim of the Society was to discuss scientific problems in different disciplines. The new scientific corporation was to contribute to "the multiplication of all sciences, to extend light, and to develop the art, industry and skills of the nation". The Rectors of the University were elected as Chairmen. The members of the Society were committed to write scientific treatises, to take part in the debates of the Society and to pay an annual fee. This new institution was, in accordance with its statute, divided into six departments, each of them grouping representatives of different sciences. Cracow itself became a subject of the studies of the new corporation of scholars and the first monographs on the history and culture of Cracow were written, and also a series of written source materials on the history of Poland was issued. Modern guides to Cracow were issued during the time when Cracow was a Free City. This series was initiated in 1822 by Ambroży Grabowski (*A Historical Description of Cracow and the Surrounding Districts*), a bookseller who was given up, heart and soul, to the past of his city. Grabowski's guide ran into six editions in the 19th century. Another very good guide-book was *A Keepsake of Cracow* (1845) by Józef Mączyński. The worthy bookseller Józef Czech issued exquisite calendars (1832—1917) sometimes containing in the informative part very valuable monographs on the history of Cracow and Poland. Ambroży Grabowski collected all the archival material he could get connected with Cracow and thus saved priceless municipal records.

A collectors' movement was also formed. Apart from private collections, mostly belonging to the aristocracy, the first museum open to the public was set up. It was organized in 1816 by Bishop Jan Paweł Woronicz, who gave halls in the bishop's palace for this purpose. The interior was much admired by his contemporaries:

"To the Pole entering this hall it seems that Clio must have opened the doors to her Temple of Memory and let him in. Wherever he looks he sees the present day and the past side by side, though divided by centuries, he opens the history book, intent and respectful and is surprised and moved at what he sees." The Historical Room was particularly moving, for it had the bones of King Boleslaus the Brave in a small reliquary. From the walls of the palace, the portraits of Poland's rulers looked down on the visitor and there were also historical pictures by Michał Stachowicz, too. That painter immortalized Kościuszko's Insurrection and the ceremonious entry of Prince Józef Poniatowski into Cracow in 1809.

The aristocrats living in Cracow imported classicist sculptures from the workshop of Antonio Canova and Bertel Thorvaldsen. From Thorvaldsen the Potocki family ordered for the Wawel Cathedral two sculptures of Christ and a monument to Włodzimierz Potocki. They are a good example of artistic sponsorship and are good classicist sculptures.

The beauty of Cracow was put on canvas by such painters as Jerzy Głowacki, Marcin Zaleski, Jan Nepomucen Głowacki and Aleksander Płonczyński. It was thanks to them that townscapes developed. It should be added here that in 1818, the School of Painting separated from the university to join up with the Institute of Technology. After this it existed for years as a School of Fine Arts. Outstanding painters worked there, such as Wojciech Korneli Stattler, Józef Brodowski, the portrait painter Józef Peszka and others. But the most outstanding artistic individuality was Piotr Michałowski. A member of the gentry, political and social worker, he studied art in the studio of Charlet in Paris. He acquainted himself with the achievements of the Romantic painters Delacroix and Géricault and equalled them with the range of his creative work. He painted with broad sweeps of the brush, scenes form the Napoleonic epic, genre scenes and some really beautiful portraits, especially those of peasants. He never treated his art as a profession, he preferred to be known as an amateur who amused himself by painting. Michałowski's paintings were ahead of his times as regards artistic form.

The Senate of the Free City set up a state theatre. In 1842, the so-called old theatre was purchased from the heirs of Jacek Kluszewski and restored. The first première in the new building of the theatre was on 1 January 1843. From that time, till the end of the 19th century, it was the only permanent theatre in the city. A Society of Friends of Music was also set up, which from 1817 was engaged in organizing concerts. Foreign virtuosi were invited to perform there. In 1843, Franz Liszt gave a concert in Cracow. In the theatre operas were performed too. Artistic criticism developed, although the reviews often pointed to the low standards of the performances.

The town-planning and architectural activity of the Senate of the Free City of Cracow is interesting in the light of the research done recently. The authorities of the Republic of Cracow continued the modernizing and town-planning activities of the Austrian authorities in the period of the occupation of Cracow (1796—1809). The Senate showed exceptional concern for the aesthetic appearance of the city. Work was finished on pulling down the defence walls. However, on the motion of Senator Feliks Radwański, the northern fragments of the fortifications, with the Barbican and Florian's Gate and the Haberdashers', Joiners' and Carpenters' bastions, were saved. In the place of the fortifications and municipal moats, a park called the Planty Gardens was laid out (1822—30). They were something new in the town-planning of the city. The squares of Cracow were put in order. The Town Hall, which was threatening collapse, was pulled down, and a new concept for the aesthetic transformation of the city was created. Cracow gradually changed into a modern city. At the same time care was taken of the historic buildings, the importance of this being quickly realized. The struggle to save the historic buildings lasted a long time. Unfortunately those in favour of preserving the architectural heritage did not succeed in saving the mediaeval fortifications and the Town Hall. On the other hand they did succeed in safeguarding the Gothic Church of St. Catherine from ruin, as well as renovating some of the buildings on Wawel Hill. The Church of SS. Peter and Paul was renovated and the convent of the Poor Clares was reconstructed. It was planned to rebuild many of the houses and to make town-planning changes to the squares of Cracow. In 1830, a Committee for Repairs to the Cracow Castle was called into being. According to the plans drawn up by the architect Francesco Maria Lanci, it was intended to rebuild the royal residence in neo-Gothic style that was fashionable at the time. However these plans were frustrated by the outbreak of the November

Insurrection. The neo-classical designs of Sebastian Sierakowski, Szczepan Humbert, Ignacy Hercok, Feliks Radwański, August Plasque and Michał Wąsowicz have been preserved in archives and provide examples of what a keen interest the Senate of the Free City of Cracow took in architectural problems. It is also a testimony to the great aesthetic culture of the people responsible for the external appearance of the city. The architecture of that period should be assessed positively. A stop was put to this lively and all-round cultural activity by the above-mentioned tragic events of the year 1846.

THE YEARS OF REGRESSION
(1846—64)

Cracow was a very sad sight at the end of 1846. The population's spirit was broken. Hundreds of arrested persons filled the prisons. Trade stopped dead. The city was feeling the Austrian occupation very acutely. The previous thirty years had the inhabitants of Cracow used to freedom and liberal and patriotic tendencies.

After the Austrians had marched into Cracow, sharp customs and passport rules were introduced, which caused an economic depression. Many merchants simply went bankrupt. Those who survived the worst period had to change their business partners, giving up the west European ones and taking on Austrian ones. The dismissal of workers from their jobs caused poverty and a high death rate.

The streets were filled with poor people and beggars. As a professor of the university, Fryderyk Hechel, wrote in 1847, "It is a sad and painful thing to go out into the streets or outside the city. In almost every corner one sees emaciated women lying on the pavement, or children who beg for pity... Every ten steps you take you come across someone moaning with hunger or illness."

Added to the revolutionary events there were bad crops and, as a result, hunger. The mortality rate rose at a frightening pace. The city was filled with mourning and the Cracovians fell into a state of torpor. Honoré de Balzac, who visited Cracow in 1847, called it "the corpse of a capital" (la cadavre de la capitale).

At the end of 1846 the disputed problem of Cracow was settled and it was given to Austria. Out of the area of the former Free City of Cracow a Grand Duchy of Cracow and the City of Cracow were made. The Commissioner of the new Duchy was Count Maurycy Deym. In Cracow, the Austrian system of administration was introduced with a Regional Office heading it. Polish civil servants were replaced by German ones. Trade was subject to customs duties and a state monopoly on salt, tobacco, saltpetre and gunpowder was introduced. The Germanization of the Jagiellonian University was started; at the same time the activity of the police was more severe. In 1846, the number of people arrested was so large that they were kept not only in prison but also in the monasteries of the Paulites, the Bernardines and Dominicans. Very severe sentences were passed. Hundreds of young people were sent to the Austrian citadels of Kufstein and Spielberg.

Amidst this progressive terror, from the beginning of 1848, there came encouraging news from the West. The Cracovians were most encouraged when they read the press information about the revolutionary occurrences in Milan, Palermo, Naples and Munich. On 22 February, the revolution broke out in Paris and Louis-Philippe was overthrown. Thus began the Revolution of 1848 or the Springtime of the Nations. Moods of excitement quickly embraced Cracow. The anti-democratic policy of the hated Metternich was loudly criticized. Shortly after this came the news that the all-powerfull Metternich had fallen. The Emperor Ferdinand promised liberal reforms and the forming of a Constituent Assembly. The prisons of Cracow were opened in mid-March and the victims of the brutal conduct of the police were carried into the streets. The next events were quick to follow. Political emigrés returned to the city from the west. Revolutionary sentiments grew. On 28 March a Citizens' Committee was called into being, the National Guard having been set up earlier. Patriotic feelings grew day by day. The radicalization of moods could be observed especially among the plebeian masses. On 24 April, the emperor announced the abolition of feudal service.

The events of 25 and 26 April constituted the culminating point of the Springtime of the Nations in Cracow. Earlier, the Austrians had already begun military preparations. They strengthened patrols, brought cannon to the city and it was forbidden to light the streets and houses at night. To make matters worse, Starost Krieg had ordered that all non-Austrians were to be stopped at the frontier. They were forced unconditionally to go back to where they had come from. The news of what the Austrians were doing made the Cracovians bitter and became the direct reason for the outbreak of the revolution. On 25 April everything was at boiling point. Heated discussions were held about the emigrés. The streets were filled with people, who were demonstrating against such practices. Krieg did not want to withdraw his order. The next day the fighting began. General Castiglione issued an order to fire at the National Guard and the demonstrators. The people built barricades, but the battle was uneven. The streets were covered with the dead. The Austrians withdrew to Wawel Hill, and from there they started the bombardment of Cracow. Roofs were ablaze, dead and injured were falling. In the meantime, the National Committee sent a delegation to Wawel Hill with the aim of negotiating with General Castiglione. General Moltke, who conducted the talks, imposed hard conditions of capitulation. The Poles had to commit themselves to the immediate dissolution of the National Committee, the disarming of the National Guard, the pulling down of barricades, payment for all damage done and the removal of the emigrés from the city. After the capitulation many persons left Cracow. The Cracovians continued to follow the news coming in from Budapest and Vienna. Many of the university students joined the Hungarian army, that was fighting against the Austrians. In Cracow, an Administrative Council of the Grand Duchy of Cracow was formed headed by Piotr Michałowski. In the city a Municipal Council was set up and the Polish language was again used in municipal documents.

At the same time, the gentry and part of the wealthy burghers began to make loyalist moves towards the new emperor Francis Joseph I, seeking ways of reaching a compromise with the Habsburg monarchy. On 9 December 1848 an act of homage, signed by the aristocrats of Cracow, was placed in the hands of the monarch. A similar programme was proclaimed by the Cracow daily *Czas*, founded in 1848 by Paweł Popiel, Adam Potocki, Kazimierz Wodzicki and Leon Rzewuski. For many years, until the days after the First World War, *Czas* was the organ of the conservatives. In 1849, the Cracovians were still following the Hungarian developments. In connection with the development of the military situation on the Hungarian front, Russian troops were marching through Cracow in May and June, on their way to assist the Austrians. Those were the last moments of the European revolution: the Springtime of the Nations was dying.

In 1849—59, there was a return to absolutism in the Habsburg monarchy, under the government of Bach. The Administrative Council was dissolved and was again replaced by a Regional Office. The Municipal Council was also abolished. The German language was again brought back for official documents. Professors who were popular with the students were removed from the university and severe censorship was introduced.

The defeat of Austria in the War of Italian Independence (1859) suddenly changed the social and political situation of Galicia. Bach was replaced in Vienna by a Pole, Agenor Gołuchowski, who started a number of social reforms. On 20 October 1860, the emperor Francis Joseph proclaimed the "October Diploma", which envisaged provincial Seyms for the whole country. And further concessions were expected.

Meanwhile, in Warsaw revolutionary sentiments were growing against Russia. In Cracow, waves of demonstrations began (1861), patriotic services were held in the churches. Maria Estreicher described these events as follows: "The services had hardly finished, when patriotic feelings found an outlet in a great pilgrimage to Mogiła during the church fair on the occasion of the feast of the Exaltation of the Holy Cross (14 September). And on 18 September, after the Mass in the Church on the Sand, an exceptionally long procession of pilgrims started out: when the beginning of the procession was coming up to the turnpike, the end of it was only just in the Floriańska [Florian's] Gate, and as more pilgrims joined the procession on the way, one can assume that a dozen or so thousand people took part in the pilgrimage, and the procession was about a quarter of a mile long. Women in black and girls in white carried little altars. They were singing the hymn *God Who Hath Protected Poland*. Ambroży Grabowski wrote afterwards in a letter to his daughter that in the 64 years he had lived in Cracow he had never seen anything more beautiful or moving. In front of the church at Mogiła, to the accompaniment of patriotic songs, a cross was driven into the ground to commemorate the Warsaw events, but shortly afterwards the gendarmerie erased the inscription on it." Underground conspiratorial organizations were ever more active. All this led in the end to the outbreak of another national insurrection. The fighting started in January 1863. The territory where the insurrection took place was the Polish Kingdom under Russian rule. When the January Insurrection started, patriotic sentiments in Cracow became stronger. Young men were recruited to partisan detachments. They intended to go and assist the insurrectionists, for the border of the Polish Kingdom was only a few kilometres from the city. Civil assistance was organized: medicines, material and medical aid. Of course, the Austrian government had to take sharp measures against this activity, not wanting to fall into conflict with Russia. The number of arrests increased. Apart from the municipal authorities there was a secret insurrectionist organization in the city, headed by Adolf Aleksandrowicz, Alfred Szczepański and Father Adam Słotwiński. There was also a secret national treasury, secret police, and postal service. After the suppression of the insurrection (1864), many of the insurrectionists came through Cracow to escape abroad. In February, the governor of Galicia proclaimed a state of siege in the country. Then started arrests and many inhabitants of the city were sent away. The city began to look deserted. In Poland there began another stage of national mourning. From Warsaw there came menacing news of the massacre of Poles and mass deportations into Russia, to Siberia. This closed another act of the history of Poland and Cracow.

Among the political auctionings, disputes and struggles, life in Cracow slowly went on. The terrible fire that swept the city in July 1850, almost razed to the ground the southern part of the town. The losses were a million zlotys and trade and cultural life disappeared for several years. The fire consumed rich church collections, archives and libraries. The valuable works of art in the churches of the Franciscans and the Dominicans were lost, too. The bishop's palace was burnt, together with the collection left by Bishop Jan Paweł Woronicz. But soon the reconstruction of the burnt part of the city was started. Many craftsmen were brought there, mainly experts on building. The churches of the Franciscans and the Dominicans were reconstructed. At the same time the Austrians made Cracow a fortress (1850) and in the plans of the Austrian staff, Cracow was to be a fortress safeguarding the frontier with Prussia. The city was surrounded with a system of bastion fortifications. From that time on, Cracow could not expand outside these fortifications.

THE GALICIAN AUTONOMY
(1867—1914)

The defeat of Austria in the war with Prussia (1866) speeded up the process of creating autonomy for Galicia, which had already lasted for many years. After losing the battle of Sadova (1866), Austria ceased to be a leading German power. From that time Prussia took over hegemony among the German states of central Europe. As a result of these events, inside the Habsburg monarchy there was opposition from the nations living under the sceptre of Francis Joseph I. Autonomy was demanded by the Bohemians, the Hungarians and the Poles. There was a repetition of the situation of 1848 and there was a threat of armed insurrections. To prevent the further development of events, Austria changed her internal policy giving up absolutist and centralized government and taking the road of liberalism.

One important aspect of this was the transformation of the absolutist monarchy into the Dual Monarchy of Austria Hungary (1867). The decree of 21 December described the social system of the monarchy as a constitutional state, and the different provinces received autonomy. This wise political manoeuvre prevented the disintegration of the empire.

Autonomy was also given to Galicia. A local parliament was introduced and a government and the post of governor. The National Seym decided on questions of culture, public building, charitable institutions and had the right of legislative initiative in the field of the general problems of the Monarchy. Lvov where the chief offices were situated became the capital of the province. An intense Polonization of Galicia was initiated. Poles again took over official posts. But authority in Galicia was taken over by the gentry and the aristocrats. The whole of the governing apparatus, subordinated to the central authorities in Vienna, was handed over to them. From the very beginning the conservative camp conducted a policy of loyalty towards the emperor and was completely satisfied with autonomy. Obviously, the conservative camp was placing its hopes exclusively in the monarchy of the Habsburgs. An important role was played in this process by the Cracovians concentrated round the daily *Czas*. Cracow became the mainstay of the Galician conservatives, in opposition to the more liberal Lvov. In the Cracow milieu, the notorious "Stańczyk's Portfolio" (1869) which constituted the political creed of the conservatives, was published. It condemned all attempts at opposition to the partitioning powers and recognized loyalty as a political programme. A faction of the Cracow conservatives gained at that time the name of the "Stańczyk Group". Tadeusz Boy-Żeleński, years afterwards, recalled the specific structure of the political forces in Cracow: "The political party commonly known as the Stańczyk Group, was born of a combination of two defeats: the suppression of the January insurrection in 1863 and the defeat of Austrians, decimated by the Prussians in the battle of Sadova in 1866. The suppression of the insurrection wiped out for a long time all dreams of independence and made people seek cooperation with the partitioning powers. The defeat of Austria caused this monarchy, consisting of various countries, to seek reconciliation with these countries by giving them wide autonomy, language and administrative freedoms. In this situation, the most influential circles found themselves a role to play, associating their natural inclinations with the dictates of sober policy: to gather round the throne in recognition of the grace of the monarchy and in this nearness to the throne consolidate their position in the country as the leading class." The representatives of this group occupied the highest positions, university chairs, etc, until 1914. They had a big influence on the intelligentsia. Cracow became a specific kind of "aristocratic settlement". The political life of the city was shaped by the influence of that conservative group. It was not until 1861 that the liberal daily *Nowa Reforma* (at the beginning it was called *Reforma*) which was in opposition to the conservative *Czas,* was published for the first time. This marked the beginning of the liberal opposition. From that time, both dailies conducted heated polemical discussions concerning problems of independence, the scope of autonomy and attitudes to national insurrections. These clashes gave tone to the political life of Cracow.

At the beginning of Cracow's autonomy it gained its own statute (1866), by virtue of which a municipal council was called into being. It had 60 members, who were elected for a period of six years, but they were elected in such a way that half of the members left the council every three years. The council elected the president of the city. In the second half of the 19th century Cracow was lucky in having excellent presidents: Józef Dietl, Mikołaj Zyblikiewicz, and at the beginning of the 20th century, Juliusz Leo. These wise men mapped out the long-term development of the city. They turned Cracow into a modern metropolis and the spiritual capital of Poland. They organized a modern administration and called into being a number of institutions that the city needed. The activity of the presidents of the period of autonomy was written in gold letters in the national culture.

In the 1880's the organized workers' movement became a social force to be reckoned with. The first socialist propaganda in Cracow came in the middle of the 1870's and coincided with the arrival in Galicia of Ludwik Waryński, a leader of the workers' movement, who escaped from the Russian partition zone in 1878. Shortly afterwards Waryński and his comrades were tried for socialist activity. The trial took place in 1880 and became quite notorious. The sentences were relatively lenient. Waryński got seven days arrest and an order to leave Austria Hungary. In the following years socialist activity intensified. The slogans proclaimed by the socialists evoked a lively echo. From 1892 the Cracow workers could join the Galician Social Democratic Party.

Cracow took the lead in the Galician socialist movement. The main ideologist and leader of the movement was the outstanding speaker Ignacy Daszyński. He launched the theory that the socialist system should be built by a gradual introduction of legal reforms. He was far from being a member of the revolutionary trend. From 1 January 1892, the socialists began to issue their own paper *Naprzód*. The paper devoted the most space to criticism of the undemocratic election system of Galicia. Social and economic relations were also criticized, and May Day marches were also started (1892). After the suppression of the Russian revolution in 1905, not only political emigrés from the Polish Kingdom came to Cracow, but also emigrés from Russia. People were attracted by the considerable political freedom. One of the visitors to the city was Vladimir I. Lenin (1912), who gave several lectures on analysis of the socialist movement in Europe. In the period just before the outbreak of the First World War, the socialists took a clearly less oppositional attitude towards the Austrian authorities. Together with the conservatives and liberals, they saw, in the rapprochement between Poland and the Austro-Hungarian monarchy, the only chance of a favourable solution to the Polish cause. Their programme envisaged the formation of a triple monarchy, in which, alongside Austria and Hungary, Galicia would be a permanent element, and which in the future the Russian zone would join. No consideration was given to the zone under Prussian rule. The Cracow socialists gave active support to the secret Union of Active Struggle which was set up in 1908, and from 1910 was transformed into an open mass paramilitary organization — Strzelec (Rifleman). It was headed by a member of the Polish Socialist Party, Józef Piłsudski, Young people joined this organization *en masse*, recognizing military training as the only way to the future struggle for independence. The main enemy was Russia, which had been hated for generations as the oppressor of the Poles. As a result, shortly before the outbreak of the First World War, Cracow became the most important centre of political life in the whole of Poland. Political and paramilitary activity was concentrated there. The riflemen's detachments trained by Józef Piłsudski were ready to take part in a war. The aim of the future attack was to be the Polish Kingdom, in which it was intended to incite an insurrection and thus separate it from Russia. Everyone was waiting for the outbreak of war, in the belief that an independent Poland would arise. It was in Cracow that Józef Piłsudski said, after the end of the war: "Cracow, let us remember, is not only a huge, enchanted, tomb of a great Nation, that catches at the heart... Cracow is a modern, great city and one of the capitals of Poland. Cracow is distinguished from other towns by the fact that it was always easier to establish cooperation with people and parties here." In such an atmosphere it was possible to set up paramilitary organizations, train people to have national consciousness and to think of the future of the Motherland.

On 1 August 1914, came the outbreak of the First World War. Cracow became an operational base for the troops of Józef Piłsudski. On 6 August Piłsudski, with a riflemen's company, marched into the Polish Kingdom. Shortly afterwards, on 16 August, the Supreme National Committee was called into being under the aegis of President Juliusz Leo. It was a political institution, representing the concept of creating Poland on the basis of Austria. By an understanding with the Austrian authorities, the Polish Legions were formed, and the command of the first brigade was entrusted to Józef Piłsudski. The legions were subordinated to the Austrian army. In 1915, Austrian troops with the allied German army took the Polish Kingdom. On 5 November a proclamation was issued from the emperors Francis Joseph and William II about the creation of a vaguely described Polish Kingdom from the lands "seized from Russian rule". This newly created state was, of course, under the protectorate of Germany and Austria. A Regency Council was even set up. Shortly after this came the day so long awaited, the day that brought Poland and Cracow freedom. The First World War was coming to an end. The period of Austrian rule came to an end. In spite of everything it can by no means be assessed negatively. Seen against the Russian and Prussian zones of rule, which witnessed a constant wave of sharp Russification and Germanization combined with political repressions and deportations, the history of the Austrian zone grew into a synonym of liberalism and Polishness. For the period of autonomy brought a liberalization of political relations, freedom to exchange views and gave Cracow a place in the foreground of the history of the nation.

THE INTELLECTUAL AND ARTISTIC CULTURE
OF CRACOW BETWEEN 1867 AND 1914

When, after 1866, the Germanization pressure was lifted and there was a long period of greater political freedom than in the other partition zones Cracow won the honourable name of "the Polish Athens". The city became the place of pilgrimage and Cracow science, art and the cultivation of patriotic traditions exerted an influence on the imagination of the generation born and brought under a foreign yoke.

Cracow was also known for its magnificent organization of patriotic ceremonies, the integrating role of which in Polish culture cannot be overestimated. In 1869, the tomb of Casimir the Great was uncovered by chance. The monarch was given a second impressive funeral which changed into a patriotic demonstration. His fellow-countrymen were reminded of the days when Poland played the role of a great power. The news of the finding and opening of the tomb of Casimir the Great spread like lightning all over the country, electrifying the people, who were dejected after the fall of the January Insurrection. "The feelings this news aroused all over the country, just cannot be described..." wrote the novelist Józef Ignacy Kraszewski, "... This appearance, amidst the living, of a great king, legislator, reformer... on the tomb of mutilated Poland, with his remains turned into ashes, with the last Polish crown and our royal sceptre... had in it something mystically influencing the people, as though by evoking with a remembrance of the past, a belief in the future." Then came the time of the next ceremonies: 1879 — the jubilee of Józef Ignacy Kraszewski's work as a writer, combined with the opening of the National Museum; 1880 — the first national congress of Polish historians, connected with the 400th anniversary of the death of Jan Długosz; 1883 — the 200th anniversary of the relief of Vienna; 1890 — the funeral of Adam Mickiewicz on Wawel Hill, and eight years later, the unveiling of a monument to the great poet; 1900 — the 500th anniversary of the reneval of the Jagiellonian University; and finally just before the outbreak of the First World War, the 500th anniversary (1910) of the victory over the Teutonic Knights in the memorable battle of Grunwald. The last-mentioned occasion turned into an organized anti-German demonstration and a monument was unveiled to King Ladislaus Jagiełło (the Grunwald Memorial), presented to the city by Ignacy Paderewski with the following eloquent inscription on the plinth: "To the glory of our fore-fathers and courage to our brothers."

All the above-mentioned ceremonies contributed to the spread of patriotism and the strengthening of the national spirit. In the shade of the church spires and the walls of Wawel, a cult of the past was born, of respect for national anniversaries and relics, which are a source of national consciousness and identity.

"In the old times," wrote a Cracow historian Stanisław Windakiewicz, "before today's Poland was born, it was the only place where thoughts of another Poland than that, which we have left behind us, came to people. From under the funeral shroud came a different reality from that with which the community was surrounded."

In the second half of the 19th century, there was another period of great intellectual movement in Cracow. Scholars concentrated round the university and the Cracow Learned Society, which as early as 1856 had separated from the Almae Matris, started independent activity which brought very satisfactory results. In the period before the gaining of autonomy, editorial work and excellent care of historic buildings was conducted by the Society, Museum collections were formed (1861), which in time became the nucleus of today's Archaeological Museum and the collection of books increased considerably as the years passed. But the Cracow Learned Society did not manage to attain a national character. After many years of discussion an institution was born in Cracow that was to link all Polish scholars. In 1872, the Cracow Learned Society was replaced by the Academy of Learning. Scholars and scientists from all the partition zones joined it and contacts were established with nearly the whole world. The Academy of Learning opened its own agencies in Rome and Paris. The fate of this Polish institution was inseparably linked with the scholars of Cracow. The community reacted keenly to the calling into being of the Academy and both generous grants and modest contributions flowed into its maintenance fund. This was a beautiful page in the history of the generosity of the public for the development of learning.

The role of the Academy of Learning and its importance depended to a great extent on the development of the Jagiellonian University. Cracow scholars had won priority among Polish scholars for many years in Polish science. The fame of the university attracted large numbers of young people to Cracow. The arts developed in a spectacular way, among them history, which is quite understandable in the period of the partitions. A great deal of emphasis was placed on critical editions of the sources for Polish history.

It was at this time that the Cracow history school was set up. Its representatives (Walerian Kalinka, Józef Szujski, Michał Bobrzyński) were critical of the history of Poland until the period of the partitions, seeing the reasons for the fall of the Commonwealth of the Gentry in the national faults and character of the Poles. Many times this extreme criticism was taken issue with by younger scholars. The Cracow school of art history also came into being at this time, its representatives being Władysław Łuszczkiewicz, Marian Sokołowski, and the younger researchers: Stanisław Tomkowicz, Julian Pagaczewski and Feliks Kopera, not all of them associated with the Jagiellonian University. Against the background of the development of the historical sciences the school for the conservation of historic monuments was set up, too. The Group of Conservators of West Galicia united historians of art, archaeologists and architects. Conservation of the Royal Cathedral on Wawel Hill was then being carried out (1895—1910) and it became a national conservation problem. Another important event was the purchase from the Austrians of the Wawel Castle and the commencement of its conservation.

Among outstanding representatives of the legal sciences were Władysław Leopold Jaworski, Fryderyk Zoll, Stanisław Wróblewski and Stanisław Estreicher. Lawyers left the university to work in the national administration and at the bar. It would be difficult not to mention such philologists and linguists as Jan Baudouin de Courtenay, Jan Michał Rozwadowski and Jan Łoś who were connected with the University. Stanisław Tarnowski was engaged in studies on Polish literature. Quite a lot of successes were noted by Polish medicine. Professor Józef Dietl was the creator of modern balneological treatment, applying for the first time the climatic treatment of pulmonary tuberculosis. Ludwik Teichmann made a study of pathological anatomy and Napoleon Cybulski had considerable achievements in the field of physiology. In the exact sciences, the physicists Zygmunt Wróblewski and Karol Olszewski attained world fame (1883, liquefaction of oxygen and nitrogen). August Witkowski conducted experiments in the field of low temperatures and his colleague at the university, Marian Smoluchowski, did studies on the thermal conductivity of gases. Leon Marchlewski did some research in the field of the structures of chlorophyll and blood, and had quite considerable success in this field. It would be difficult to mention all the names of people who boosted science in Cracow and marked out the way for further development.

A separate page in Polish culture and science belongs to the Cracow family of the Estreichers, who were associated with the University since the days when Kołłątaj introduced his reforms there. As has already been said, the first member of this merited family came to Cracow in 1777 from Iglau in Moravia. Kołłątaj intended to entrust the Chair of Drawing and Painting to him. The Polonization of the family was as quick as lightning. In 1868, Karol Estreicher became the director of the university library (Jagiellonian Library). He was responsible for the issue of a monumental publication "Polish Bibliography" (Bibliografia polska), the first volume of which appeared in 1871. The Estreichers' Bibliography contains the whole of the achievements of Polish writers, beginning with the 15th century up to the 20th century.

This work was continued by Karol's son, Stanisław Estreicher, a world famous lawyer, then by Karol Estreicher junior, a historian of art and also a professor at the university, who died in 1984.

In the period when Cracow gained autonomy, there was also a development of elementary and secondary schools. In addition to the Academy of Learning, other institutions of great importance for Poland were set up. Towards the end of the century (1896) the municipal archives, which possessed a full set of documents issued since the 14th century, were opened to researchers.

A large number of museums were also opened. In 1876, Prince Władysław Czartoryski presented Cracow with an invaluable family collection of works of art, gathered from the end of the 18th century. Among the paintings there were works by Leonardo da Vinci, Raphael and Rembrandt. In addition to the Czartoryski Museum, he also handed over a large library and a collection of archive documents. But the leading role was played by the National Museum, which was set up in 1879. It was a museum of a national character, according to the principles on which it was set up. The aim of the National Museum was to collect relics showing the historical and artistic past of the whole nation. Polish art was collected and it was included in the sphere of European culture. The first director to be nominated was the outstanding historian of art Władysław Łuszczkiewicz (d. 1900), and he was followed for several dozen years by Feliks Kopera (d. 1952). The collections of the Museum, mainly Polish paintings from Gothic times to the present day, were shown to the public. The first permanent exhibition was opened in 1883. Shortly afterwards (1902), the National Museum gained the valuable numismatic collection of Count Emeryk Hutten-Czapski, and later other collections too.

Artistic life was concentrated round the Society of Friends of Art (1854). All the exhibitions of sculptures, paintings and graphic art were organized by the Society of Friends of Art. Research into Cracow and its past was conducted successfully (from 1896) by the Society of Friends of the History and Architectural Heritage of Cracow, to which many outstanding scholars belonged. From the very beginning it began to issue *The Cracow Library* and *The Cracow Yearbook*. These publications, which are still appearing today, contain the whole of our knowledge about the past of Cracow.

The 1890's, when art nouveau flourished, brought a turning point in the artistic history of the city. But before it came to this the art in Cracow developed in the all-European stream of historicism, which penetrated into every artistic phenomenon, beginning with architecture. The area of the city was limited by the Austrian fortifications, which marked out the maximum line of building. The boundaries of Cracow in those times were approximately within a circle about 1 to 1.5 km. from the Market Place. Dense building only went up to the line of the Planty Gardens. But the change of the course of the River Vistula gave new areas for building houses in the eastern part of the city (Dietla Street and the surrounding area). At the same time new streets were opened in the area of the former Garbary, Kleparz, Stradom and Kazimierz. All the buildings put up represented the prevailing historical style, from neo-Gothic, neo-Renaissance through neo-Baroque up to eclecticism. Outstanding architects worked on the expansion of the city, most of them educated at German and Austrian universities: Feliks Księżarski (Collegium Novum of the Jagiellonian University), Filip Pokutyński (the building of the Academy of Learning), Maciej Moraczewski (the building of the Academy of Fine Arts), Tomasz Pryliński (the renovation of Cloth Hall, the buildings of the Society for Mutual Insurance and the building founded by the Helcel family), Jan Zawiejski (the Słowacki Theatre), Teodor Talowski (houses in Retoryka Street). Altogether, monumental architecture was built, rich in details and satisfactory as regards technique, not in any way different from what was being built in Prague, Budapest or Vienna at the same time. The present city of Cracow is mostly architecture from the period of Galician autonomy. It determines the aspect of many streets in Cracow.

Sculpture remained faithful to the classicist trend: the work of Oskar Sosnowski (the monuments to Jadwiga and Jagiełło in the Planty Gardens, the figure of Father Piotr Skarga in the Church of SS. Peter and Paul), Walery Gadomski (the statue of Nicolaus Copernicus in the hall of the Academy of Learning) and Alfred Daun, author of the sculptures in the Planty Gardens (Grażyna, Lilla Weneda). The competition for a monument to Adam Mickiewicz had a wide impact. In the end the one chosen for realization was the not very good design of Teodor Rygier. The monument to the national bard was unveiled in 1898, on the hundredth anniversary of the birth of the poet. Good form is represented by the works of Antoni Madeyski, whose sarcophagi to Queen Jadwiga and King Ladislaus of Varna in the Wawel Cathedral, were executed at the beginning of the 20th century. At the beginning of the present century, Cyprian Godebski created the monuments to Copernicus (opposite the university) and Aleksander Fredro (opposite the Słowacki Theatre). From distant Rome, the works of Pius Weloński were brought. He created for   94

Cracow the monument to Bohdan Zaleski in the Planty Gardens and the Monument to Cardinal Jerzy Radziwiłł in the Cathedral.

But the prime place in art was taken by the Cracow painters. The talented Jan Matejko (1838—93) grew out of the atmosphere of the Cracow of the past.

His deep and well thought out visions of history influenced the whole of Polish society with his patriotic subjects. There was hardly a single historical event that Matejko did not paint. His pictures served the teaching of history and were also a means of giving courage to the people. They taught about and also warned against the faults and errors of the nation. The great historical compositions of Matejko (*Prussian Homage, Báthory at Pskov, Skarga's Sermon, Rejtan, The Constitution of May 3rd* and *Kosciuszko at Racławice*) created stereotypes of historical thought and were greatly admired. Matejko and his role can only be compared with the work of the Romantic poets Adam Mickiewicz and Juliusz Słowacki. Matejko has been the only Polish painter fully accepted by the Polish nation. His paintings were known from reproductions by the whole of Poland. He was generally accepted as the artistic leader of the nation. Conscious of his mission, he painted mainly historical pictures, ignoring the fashionable trends in art. Apart from painting historical compositions and portraits, Matejko also painted a beautiful mural polychrome in St. Mary's Church. This work excellently plays off the mediaeval architecture of the church. Matejko for many years was head of the Academy of Fine Arts in Cracow. He trained a large number of pupils, who continued his work, without paying attention to the fundamental changes that were taking place in European art. The individuality of Matejko left its stamp on the artistic development of his pupils. After his death (1893), Cracow painters were to take quite a different path, under the influence of western trends.

While Matejko was still alive, his best pupils left for Paris to study the new art. For the echoes of the new art (art nouveau) were coming to Cracow from Paris and Vienna. The whole of Europe was experiencing great changes in art. In Paris, impressionism had been fully accepted, in Vienna, Sezessionstil had been born. Artistic life moved from the academy to coffee houses, where, amidst the smoke of cigarettes and the fragrant smell of coffee, views were exchanged on art. Cracow was not to be left behind, and like the whole of Europe was experiencing years of intellectual ferment, the period of *Fin de siècle*. Cracow was living through its great period in art, it was the capital of the artistic movement that was known as Young Poland, or Modernism. The Bohemian circles were experiencing a triumph. But let facts speak for themselves.

Not long after the death of Matejko, Julian Fałat, an outstanding landscape painter, became the director of the Academy of Fine Arts. He opened the walls of the Academy to new artistic trends. Shortly afterwards, the Academy of Fine Arts (so named in 1900) became a really modern higher school. In 1895, Stanisław Wyspiański, who had just returned from Paris, began to paint polychromes in the Franciscan church. His stained glass windows and the above mentioned polychrome murals, are marked for their fluid art nouveau lines. A fundamental date in the culture of the period under review was the formation in 1897 of the "Art" association of artists and the first issue of the paper *Życie* (Life). Young artists quickly gathered around *Życie*. Kazimierz Tetmajer printed his poetry in that periodical and polemical articles were published on art and its functions. Slogans of idealism, symbolism and pure form were launched.

Stanisław Przybyszewski was shortly to rule the souls of the Cracovians. He came there from Germany in 1898. Enveloped in the legend of a man of genius and the fame of a good poet, he began working in Cracow where he at once shocked people with his bohemian style of living, his temperament and various social scandals. Young artists quickly found in him a twin soul and were the constant companions of his and his beautiful Norwegian wife Dagny Juel. Most often they gathered in the Paon café run by Turliński. Here, till daybreak, they discussed problems of literature and painting. Pure form was sought in art and poetry. Articles written by Przybyszewski were published in *Życie* and caused a lot of commotion among artists.

But of the greatest significance for Cracow were the works of Stanisław Wyspiański (1869—1907), poet, dramatist and painter. He was born in Cracow, and from his earliest years was fascinated with the past of the city which he loved dearly. His literary works were near to the traditions of the great Romantics and were devoted to vital problems of national existence.

Cracow played a primary role in the creative work of Wyspiański. The artist brought to life the historical figures of Boleslaus the Bold, Bishop Stanislaus Szczepanowski, and Casimir the Great, creating visions of the Poland of the past. His writings were accompanied by pictures he painted. A lover of the antique came to life in the works of the poet, but always he put Cracow first in his poems, and also royal Wawel, which he identified with Poland: In the play *Deliverance* he wrote as follows:

"Here everything is Polish, every stone and every crumb, and the man who appears here becomes a part of Poland... You are surrounded by an Eternal Poland; which is immortal for ever."

Wyspiański also managed to agitate public opinion in Cracow. His play *The Wedding Party* was an account of the authentic wedding of a poet and friend of the writer, Lucjan Rydel, who married a daughter of a peasant from Bronowice. The play was actually a reckoning with the contemporary intelligentsia: all the characters had their own counterparts in real life, which was the reason for the social scandals. The artistic power of *The Wedding Party* has lasted till this very day.

The poet was very attached to the Cracow theatre, which at the turn of the 19th and 20th centuries became an important disseminator of culture, cultivating the excellent traditions from the second half of the previous century. It was in Cracow that the magnificent actress, Helena Modrzejewska (Modjeska), began her stage career. Wyspiański was fascinated by the stage from his childhood. The years 1899—1905 were the most glorious period of the Cracow theatre, which coincided with the creative activity of Wyspiański. His dramas were staged there and Wyspiański did everything by himself, the staging and all the details were all his work. His versatility matched that of the artists of the Renaissance period, and Wyspiański became an artistic phenomenon at the turn of the century. He was laid to rest in the crypt of honoured Poles in the Church on the Cliff. His funeral was a huge demonstration of homage to the artist.

Next to Wyspiański there were many other outstanding artists who passed through Cracow. Such famous painters as Jacek Malczewski (1854—1929), Jan Stanisławski (1860—1900), Józef Mehoffer (1869—1946), Leon Wyczółkowski (1852—1936), Wojciech Weiss (1875—1950), and Włodzimierz Tetmajer (1862—1923) decided the kind of art of their times. The Academy of Fine Arts became the most progressive artistic school. As regards sculptors, the most eminent were Karol Hukan (1898—1958), Konstanty Laszczka (1865—1956) and Xawery Dunikowski (1875—1964), the greatest of them all, who had a considerable influence on modern Polish sculpture. Applied art also flourished, taking a lot of its motifs from Polish nature and folk art. Stained glass design, graphic art and decoration of books also developed. The tastes of the people changed under the influence of the art nouveau period, and this style prevailed generally in interior decoration. Quite an important role was played here by the Polish Applied Art Society.

Some good examples of art nouveau architecture are the buildings designed by Franciszek Mączyński. His design for a Palace of Art, which is a reduced version of the Sezession Palace in Vienna (Joseph Olbrich), was completed in 1901. The Jesuit Church (1909—21), which harmoniously links mock historical elements with the art nouveau style and local building traditions, was also the work of Mączyński. He often worked with Tadeusz Stryjeński. They designed together the sumptuous building, housing the Industrial and Trade Chamber (1906), which combined elements of various epochs, but in its details was art nouveau. Both these artists were responsible for the reconstruction of the Stary Theatre (1903—05), giving it art nouveau decoration, particularly the frieze (the work of Józef Gardecki). The most original, completely art nouveau, is the decoration of the façade of the building Dom Czynciela (1907—08), executed according to the design of Ludwik Wojtyczko. Sławomir Odrzywolski, the author of the interesting building of the Industrial School (1912) and also that of the Agricultural Society, managed to combine historical motifs excellently with those of art nouveau style and folk art. Apart from the above mentioned the following architects were active in Cracow: Władysław Ekielski, Jan Zawiejski and Józef Pakies. Some of them had already passed through the phases of historical imitation, eclecticism, to design in the spirit of art nouveau. It should be mentioned here that the art nouveau elements introduced to architectural designs only concerned the details, shaping the form of the building.

It would be difficult to imagine the Cracow art in the times of the Young Poland Movement, without mention of the artistic phenomenon the "Green Balloon" cabaret. In 1895, Jan Apolinary Michalik set up the Lwowska (Lvov) Café in Floriańska Street. As it was situated by the Academy of Fine Arts, it soon became the place where artists met. The café changed its name to "Michalik's Den" and it was there, in October 1905, that the "Green Balloon" cabaret was formed. Tadeusz Boy-Żeleński, Karol Frycz, Jan August Kisielewski, Teofil Trzciński and many others participated in the programmes presented by the cabaret. Painters decorated the interior or Michalik's café and a charming fin de siècle interior was arranged with the furniture, paintings and stained glass windows all in the same style. Satirical performances were given in the café, joking about the local notables. Fun was made of the puritanical habits of the bourgeoisie. It was all excellent entertainment. There was not a single event that was not made fun of by the cabaret. It lasted until 1912. But its legend remained and this was because of Tadeusz Boy-Żeleński, who became the official historian and apologist of the "Green Balloon" cabaret. It provided a lot of rumours that shocked and scandalized some of the Cracovians. About fifty years after the forming of the "Green Balloon" cabaret, a theatre critic Jan Paweł Gawlik thus wrote about the cabaret: "It was not only the clear thinking of the 'Green Balloon' that made it so popular. It was a kind of Trojan horse, through the medium of which it was possible to penetrate to minds with the Voltairian message of the intellect. The Trojan horse was... pepper. Not salt from Attica, not refined eroticism, not frivolous elegant joke, but a joke sharp in flavour, because it had peppers generously shaken on it, between the consonants and the syllables, sentences and verses of the 'Green Balloon'. This is the secret of the popularity and the lasting character of the texts of our first literary cabaret — in which skirts were pulled up in times when there was still strict discipline, and severe customs, even if only seemingly so."

The creative achievements of Young Poland pressed a lasting stamp on the culture of Cracow, on the traditions and attitude of its inhabitants. It became to some extent the crowning of the cultural development of the city in the times of the Galician autonomy. The variety of culture in those times testifies to the talents that were developed by the former capital of the Piasts and the Jagiellons. The history of Cracow in those years is one of the most beautiful in the thousand years history of the city.

CHAPTER VII • THE DEVELOPMENT OF CRACOW IN THE 20TH CENTURY

IN INDEPENDENT POLAND (1918—39)

The Russian offensive stopped at the line of Cracow in 1914. With impatience the people observed the diplomatic bargaining over the question of Poland and watched the fortunes of war — with every passing year there was ever stronger belief in the rebirth of a free Polish state. In autumn 1918, there began to be formed in various parts of Poland, centres of the new authorities. On 31 October the Polish troops disarmed the Austrians stationed in the city — Cracow was free, the imperial eagles and German inscriptions were torn down.

In the first days of November, in Lublin, a new government was formed of socialist and peasant party leaders, headed by Ignacy Daszyński. In the middle of November, Józef Piłsudski called into being a provisional government and himself took the post of its head. There was a free Poland with its capital in Warsaw.

We shall not go into the complicated problems of Poland's politics and economics in the twenty years between the two World Wars, as we are still interested, above all, in the role and importance of Cracow, this time in a new political situation.

In the period of the Second Commonwealth, the city was one of the main centres of learning, culture and art. According to data from 1921, Cracow had a population of 184,300. In 1921, Cracow was raised to the rank of the capital of a voivodship and in 1925 a church metropolis was created there. The first metropolitan archbishop Adam Stefan Sapieha (d. 1951) was nominated. The city still fulfilled the function of a national sanctuary. The ashes of Juliusz Słowacki were buried there in 1927, in the Wawel crypts. It was also the place where, in 1935, Marshal Piłsudski was buried. Numerous excursions of people wishing to see the magnificent historic monuments and learn their national history, still go to Cracow.

At the very beginning of the new historical situation, Cracow was the scene of an economic crisis, which later spread to the whole country. The main aims of the young republic were to lead the country out of the war chaos and its consequences and to unite the economically differentiated areas, to expand the uniform administration and make the best out of the access to the sea. The new Polish state had to fight enormous economic difficulties. Financial difficulties made the inflation rate rise day by day and this brought the obvious economic results. Prices rose quicker than earnings. The sharpening situation led in 1923 to the outbreak of a workers' strike. The government was attacked because it was regarded as the only culprit responsible for the poor material situation of the working class. On 6 November street fighting took place. Eighteen people were killed and several dozen wounded. These Cracow events were just a fragment of the workers' demonstrations in the autumn of 1923.

The Cracow disturbances in 1923 were not the only ones in the two interwar decades. The Cracow workers organized another demonstration in 1936. In March, a wave of major strikes went through the whole of Poland. Sharp anti-government manifestations took place. In Cracow, the workers of the "Suchard" chocolate factory went on strike later to be joined by workers of the "Semperit" rubber goods factory. Soon a general strike was proclaimed, organized by the socialists and communists. The police opened fire on the demonstrators. There were killed and wounded. At the funeral of the murdered men (10 persons) there was an attendance of nearly 30,000 people. As a result, the workers managed to get a rise in pay, the right to hold sit-in strikes and unemployed workers were given jobs in public works. The social significance of the Cracow incidents was very large, showing once again the role of the working class in the political life of the country.

In the period under review, the focus of political life was moved to Warsaw; for it was the place of residence of the president of the state and also of the government of the Polish Republic. The main events passed Cracow by. But the city lived mainly for its culture and learning.

Scientific life was, of course, centred round the university and the Polish Academy of Learning (in 1919, the Academy was given a new name, the Polish Academy of Learning). Also in 1919 another very important higher school was opened — the Academy of Mining, which trained specialized engineers for the mining industry and metallurgical plants. The opening ceremony took place in the assembly hall of the Jagiellonian University on 10 October. Józef Piłsudski attended the ceremony. The first students graduated from the Academy of Mining in 1923. It had two departments: mining and metallurgy.

The Jagiellonian University had five faculties: law, philosophy, medicine, agriculture and theology. It employed nearly 250 professors and assistant professors. Quite a large number of them had been lecturing there since the end of the 19th century. In the fields of law and the arts, the Cracow milieu took the lead in Polish learning. The Law Department was famed for the students who studied under the following professors: Rafał Taubenschlag (Roman law), Stanisław Kutrzeba (history of law), Stanisław Estreicher (history of law) and professors lecturing on civil law: Stanisław Wróblewski, Władysław Kumaniecki and Jan Gwiazdomorski. Lectures on political economy were conducted by the eloquent lecturer Adam Krzyżanowski. Historians were represented by the mediaevalists: Jan Dąbrowski, Władysław Semkowicz and Roman Grodecki. Modern history and contemporary history was taught by scholars of such standing as Władysław Konopczyński, Józef Feldmann, Kazimierz Piwarski and Stanisław Kot, and the younger professors were Kazimierz Lepszy and Henryk Barycz. The history of Polish literature was lectured on by Ignacy Chrzanowski, Stanisław Windakiewicz and Stanisław Pigoń. Kazimierz Nitsch and Tadeusz Lehr-Spławiński were engaged in linguistics. History of art was represented by Stanisław Pagaczewski, Tadeusz Szydłowski and the young assistant professor Adam Bochnak. The Faculty of Musicology was run by the outstanding scholar Zdzisław Jachimecki. Classical philology, headed by Leon Sternbach and Tadeusz Sinko, stood very well. Romance philology was the field of Stanisław Wędkiewicz and Stanisław Folkierski. An English Philology Faculty was also set up by Roman Dyboski. Research in chemistry was conducted by Karol Dziewoński, Tadeusz Estreicher and Leon Marchlewski. Astronomy was developing well. Tadeusz Banachiewicz won world fame for his research on celestial mechanics and establishing a mathematical method for calculating the orbits of heavenly bodies, known as the Cracovian calculus. Among natural historians, Władysław Szafer, Henryk Hoyer and Michał Siedlecki all won fame.

Professors of medicine associated with the university clinics did some more practical work. Tadeusz Kostanecki did research on comparative anatomy, obtaining some very good results. Jan Glatzer won fame in Cracow as an excellent surgeon. Research was also done on the aetiology of tuberculosis (Emil Godlewski) and cancerous growths (J. W. Supniewski). Skin diseases were the speciality of the outstanding dermatologist Franciszek Walter. Józef Piltz represented a modern psychiatric school. Among the professors of medicine there was also a historian of that discipline, Władysław Szumowski. Pharmacy was also studied, under Marek Gatty-Kostyal.

In 1925, a Higher School of Commerce was opened (renamed in 1937 as the Commercial Academy), training good specialists for offices and departments.

The highest scientific institution in independent Poland was the Polish Academy of Learning, situated in Cracow. Its presidents in the two interwar decades were successively: Kazimierz Morawski, Jan Rozwadowski, Kazimierz Kostanecki and Stanisław Wróblewski. Among the publications of the Polish Academy of Learning mention is due to the monumental *Polish Biographical Dictionary*, which began to appear in 1935 and constitutes a national biography. Series of botanical books also began to appear: *Polish Flora* and *Atlas of Polish Flora*. The university and the Academy were the patrons of many learned societies: the Pedagogical Society, the Society of Friends of the Polish Language and the Society of Friends of History

and the Architectural Heritage of Cracow. An active scientific movement began to develop.

Research was carried out by the National Museum and the small Ethnographic Museum. They played a double role, that of a scientific laboratory and a place to contemplate works of art.

Cracow art was closely associated with the Academy of Fine Arts. Some of the old professors still remained after the war, to mention only Jacek Malczewski, Józef Mehoffer, Teodor Axentowicz, Wojciech Weiss and the sculptor Konstanty Laszczka. Moreover, there was a branch of the Cracow Academy in Paris, headed by Józef Pankiewicz. New chairs of painting were entrusted to young artists: Fryderyk Pautsch, Kazimierz Sichulski, Stanisław Kamocki and Stanisław Dębicki. Xawery Dunikowski became the professor of sculpture. A faculty of interior decoration was opened in 1920. Artistic ferment was provided by the painters who had attended the Paris branch of the Cracow Academy. They brought with them from Paris interest in post-impressionism and colour. Among them were Józef Jarema, Czesław Rzepiński and Józef Pankiewicz. At the same time there were formists, opposed to art nouveau. They were: Zofia Stryjeńska, Tymon Niesiołowski, Tytus Czyżewski, Zbigniew Pronaszko, Leon Chwistek and Stanisław Ignacy Witkiewicz, otherwise known as Witkacy. All the artistic trends (colourism, formism) brought a breath of fresh air with them. They cleaned Cracow of the accretions of art nouveau, and prepared the way for the birth of the artistic vanguard. In opposition to the existing artistic trends, the Group Cracow formed in 1932, was avant-garde, associated with the Communist Party of Poland. This group was among the most important artistic associations of the previous half century. It quickly gained recognition and importance. Among its members were Sasza Blonder (d. 1949), Berta Grünberg, Maria Jarema (d. 1958), Leopold Lewicki (d. 1973), Adam Marczyński, Jonasz Stern and Henryk Wiciński (d. 1943). Their art was abstract. This group of artists was connected with the avant-garde theatre "Cricot I".

Indirectly, the literary avant-garde was associated with the avant-garde of painters. Shortly after the end of the war, the first futurist works appeared in Cracow. The leading lights of the futurists were Bruno Jasieński, Tytus Czyżewski and Stanisław Młodożeniec. The theoretical foundations were given to the futurists by the painter and philosopher Leon Chwistek. But the life of this group was very short. A new phase in the avant-garde movement was started by writers and painters concentrated round the periodical *Zwrotnica* first published in 1922 by Tadeusz Peiper, a theoretician of modern poetry. They were, among others, Julian Przyboś, Jan Brzękowski, and Jalu Kurek. They did not stay together long. In 1924 Peiper suspended the issue of *Zwrotnica*. Finally, in 1927, it stopped appearing altogether. To sum up, due to internal quarrels, these representatives of the avant-garde did not have any important influence on the history of Cracow. But they did have some quite important achievements in the artistic field and demonstrated to the Cracovians the new trends in European literature.

In addition to the avant-garde, there were the groups Helion and Litart, in which writers associated with the literary press (*Gazeta Literacka* and *Wiadomości Literackie*) were active, and continued the Young Poland traditions (Antoni Waśkowski). Younger writers and poets then appeared: Józef Gałuszka, Jan Sztaudynger, Witold Zechenter, Jerzy Ronard Bujański, and Adam Polewka, who was connected with the communists.

The two interwar decades were also marked by architectural work. The expansion of Cracow, started during the period in office of Mayor Juliusz Leo, caused a number of town-planning changes, which were continued with success.

Słowackiego, Mickiewicza and Krasińskiego Avenues were built and also the western parts of the city. New villa districts were built: Cichy Kącik (Quiet Corner) snd the Officers' Estate. In architecture, monumental buildings of classicist form were the most abundant. The buildings that went up in Cracow at that time gave the city some good works of art. Among the outstanding architects who were active then were such excellent ones as Adolf Szyszko-Bohusz (d. 1946) and Wacław Krzyżanowski (d. 1954). Adolf Szyszko-Bohusz was recognized, above all, as a conservator of historic monuments, including the royal castle on Wawel Hill. Another of his works is the monumental building of the Savings Bank (1925). Also, the post-classicist trend explains the form of the building of the Mining Academy (1923—35), designed by Wacław Krzyżanowski. The same architect designed the building of the Treasury Chamber (1922—25). The building of the Bank of Poland (1921—24) is in the same style. It was designed by two architects — Teodor Hofman and Kazimierz Wyczyński. A reflection of the newest forms applied in world architecture was the building of the Jagiellonian Library (1931—39), designed by Wacław Krzyżanowski. Monumentalism is the characteristic feature of the magnificent building of the National Museum (1934—39), which was started before the war to the design by Czesław Boratyński, B. Schmidt, and Edward Kreisler. All the buildings put up before the war are characterized by their classicism, with simplified forms and restraint in the application of details, and also monumentalism. The first development of modern architecture was stopped by the outbreak of the Second World War.

THE NAZI OCCUPATION (1939—45)

At dawn, on 1 September 1939, the war started. Nazi Germany attacked Poland. The Cracovians were awakened that morning by the sound of planes and explosions of the bombs. Airfields and strategic targets were bombed. The Polish authorities were evacuated from Cracow. Thousands left their homes quickly, to wander round the country. The most valuable museum collections were also evacuated, including the Arras tapestries of King Sigismund Augustus and the Crown Treasury. They found their way to Canada during the war. Other invaluable works of art were hidden.

On 6 September, the Germans took Cracow. The German occupation lasted till 18 January 1945. On 12 October the "*General-Gouvernement für besetzten polnischen-Gebiete*" was called into being at the orders of Hitler. On 26 October, the civil administration took over from the Wehrmacht. Cracow became the capital of the General-Gouvernement. The frontiers of the General-Gouvernement were marked out in such a way that the industrialized regions of former Poland were included in the Reich, and the over-populated agricultural areas were included in the new territory.

The fact of creating Cracow as the capital of the General-Gouvernement brought a number of German officials there with their families and the police protection for Germans was doubled. Hans Frank became Governor General and chose Wawel as his residence. His deputy was Artur Seyes-Inquart, who in the spring of 1940 was replaced by Joseph Bühler. Bühler also discharged the function of the head of the government of the General-Gouvernement. Special districts were reserved for the German officials and the Polish residents were removed from them. The Gestapo persecuted the Polish population, street round-ups were organized, people were taken away for forced labour to Germany or to death camps. The Headquarters of the Gestapo in Pomorska Street became a symbol of torture and execution.

On 6 November, university professors were lured to the Collegium Novum by stratagem. They were supposed to attend a lecture given by a representative of the German authorities. On that memorable day, 186 Cracow scholars were deprived of their freedom. They were arrested and taken to the concentration camp at Oranienburg-Sachsenhausen. There, during the frosty winter of 1939—40 many of them died a martyr's death, including Antoni Meyer, Stanisław Estreicher, Stefan Bednarski, Jerzy Smoleński, Tadeusz Garbowski, Michał Siedlecki, Feliks Rogoziński, Kazimierz Kostanecki, Adam Różański, Ignacy Chrzanowski, Władysław Takliński, Antoni Hoborski, Leon Sternbach and others.

The Germans closed the Jagiellonian University, and the whole of secondary school network was abolished. All this was in accordance with the political principles of Nazism. In a speech on 31 October 1939, Hans Frank said: "We must clearly state the difference between the German nation of lords and the Poles. The Poles will from now on only be able to have such an education, which will show them the hopelessness of their existence as a nation."

But from the beginning of 1940, clandestine education was already underway. The Jagiellonian University operated underground, training new members of the Polish intelligentsia. A hundred and thirty-six lectures ran the classes of nearly 800 students. Doctoral and assistant professor's dissertations were written. Lectures were held in secret at private homes and in the flats of the professors and students. Secret learning at all levels was among the most noble work for the nation. A new intelligentsia was prepared, which saved the community from planned cultural extinction. Secret teaching was a deliberate act of sabotage against the plans of the invader.

The Germans furiously destroyed all traces of Polish culture. They took away to Germany many invaluable works of art from museums and private collections. They devastated church treasuries. From the National Museum they took the pictures of Hans Dürer, Leonardo da Vinci, Raphael. They also took the altar of Wit Stwosz from St. Mary's Church. They destroyed monuments: in 1939, the Grunwald Monument was destroyed, and in 1940, the monument to Adam Mickiewicz in the Market Place and to Thaddeus Kosciuszko on Wawel Hill. Polish names disappeared from the streets and were replaced by German ones.

As time went on the terror of the invader increased. The answer of the Poles was the gradual growth of the resistance movement. In the provinces partisans began to fight. Anti-German leaflets began to appear in the streets and secret papers were distributed. In the meantine, in Oświęcim (Auschwitz), near Cracow, the concentration camp absorbed millions of victims. Mass executions of Poles began. In 1941, the Germans created a Jewish Ghetto. The accounts given by those that survived the Ghetto are shocking. The news coming from the mass extermination camp at Oświęcim filled people with terror. With an increasing frequency transports of prisoners from Cracow were being sent there. Extermination also reached artistic milieux. On 19 April 1942, the Germans conducted a round-up at the artists' coffee house in Łobzowska Street. The arrested artists were taken to Auschwitz. They shared the fate of millions of Poles murdered in concentration camps. The year 1943 saw the liquidation of the Cracow Ghetto. Posters appeared in the streets with the names of those condemned to death.

The year 1944 was a dangerous one for Cracow. The front line was slowly getting nearer and nearer. On 8 April a list of 112 persons condemned to death was posted up in the street. From the beginning of August, news began to come through from Warsaw of the outbreak of the Uprising and the first successful battles. These gave the people fresh courage. At the news of the outbreak of the Uprising in Warsaw, the invaders organized a huge round-up (6 August 1944). Nearly 7,000 men were then arrested, some of whom were sent to concentration camps.

In the autumn, refugees began to arrive in Cracow from burning Warsaw. At the same time the front line was getting nearer the boundaries of the city. The severe winter that year was to be the last winter of occupation. In the second week of January 1945, the Red Army started its big offensive. It brought the final breakdown of the German eastern front.

The Nazis organized a bloody execution in the Cracow district of Dąbie on 15 January. Seventy-nine persons died then. The Germans, fleeing Cracow, decided to blow up the whole city, to destroy its beautiful historic buildings. In the Nazi plans, the city was to share the fate of Warsaw. The Nazis did not succeed in carrying out these plans. The Red Army flanked the city and took it with an attack from the west, surprising the enemy who thought they would attack from the east. The central switch disconnecting the mines was quickly safeguarded. This brilliant manoeuvre by the troops of Marshal Konev, saved Cracow from complete destruction. All the retreating German troops could do was to blow up the bridges over the River Vistula.

On 18 January 1945, Cracow was again free. It was the end of the nightmarish occupation night. Then came the difficult years of rebuilding Cracow from war damage.

IN THE NEW CONDITIONS (AFTER 1945)

On 21 January 1945 representatives of the Provisional Government (set up in Lublin which had been liberated by the Russians in 1944), arrived in Cracow. The country was entering the road of economic and social change. An agrarian reform was carried out and industry was nationalized. A new system of local government was introduced — people's councils. On 24 January the first meeting of the Municipal People's Council took place. The city was entering a new period of its history.

The period up to 1956 was characterized by a quick development of industry and rebuilding from the ravages of war. In 1949, the Lenin Steel Works was set up near Cracow. The building of an industrial centre was accompanied by the building of the town of Nowa Huta. People came to the new centre from little towns and villages near Cracow. In 1951, Nowa Huta was made part of Cracow. Owing to the big inflow of population it was necessary tb expand Cracow. New housing settlements were built, unfortunately of not very interesting architecture.

By a resolution of the Seym in 1955, Cracow was raised to the status of a voivodship town, separate from the surrounding territory which ensured the future development of the city. In October 1956, there was an upheaval within the ruling team. The governing group acting under the strong influence of Stalin's ideas was overthrown. In the autumn of 1956, Cracow witnessed demonstrations of students and workers who supported the change, which pleased the people. Support was given to the new political line represented by Władysław Gomułka and his governing group. After 1956, a spectacular development of culture in Cracow took place, which was accompanied by the development of industry. The city also became an industrial centre after the war, which had its negative side in that it caused pollution of the atmosphere and the natural environment. Industry has had a destructive effect on the historic buildings of Cracow.

At the same time as the political changes were taking place, there were also social changes. There was a quick increase of the population (1945 — 298,500; 1955 — 421,000; 1963 — 517,800), and as a result of this, the expansion of Cracow. New housing estates were constantly being built and the municipal communications network was also expanded. Schools and numerous educational establishments were also built.

As in the interwar period (1918—39), the life of Cracow concentrated round culture and art. Shortly after the end of the war, the higher schools resumed their activity, as did the secondary schools. The first scientific meetings of the commissions of the Polish Academy of Learning were held. Learned societies came to life again, and libraries and archives were opened. The museums also opened their doors again. At the end of April 1946, a large railway transport of works of art that had been taken away by the Germans arrived in Cracow. They were brought to Poland from the territory of the Third Reich by Professor Karol Estreicher. It was a rich harvest: the altar of Wit Stwosz from St. Mary's Church, *Lady with a Weasel* by Leonardo da Vinci, *Landscape with the Good Samaritan* by Rembrandt and many other works of art.

The years 1945 and 1946 were very important for the further cultural development of Cracow. At that time many writers, artists and theatre people came to Cracow from Warsaw which had been razed to the ground. Cracow, in those years, gave refuge to those who represented Polish literature, culture and art. It was in Cracow that all the scientific periodicals and literary papers were issued and in Cracow that the first publishing houses were set up. The city was showing again how very much alive its cultural traditions were.

The 1950's brought numerous changes in the structure of science in Cracow. Above all, the renowned Polish Academy of Learning was closed. It was replaced in 1951 by the Polish Academy of Sciences, with its headquarters in Warsaw. The old Jagiellonian University was split up. The Medical Academy was separated from it (1952) and also the Agricultural Academy (1953). The excellent Theological Department was abolished and included in the Academy of Catholic Theology in Warsaw. Earlier a Teachers' College had been set up (1946). In July 1954, the Cracow Technical University began to operate separately from the Mining and Metallurgical Academy. New higher schools were set up: the Academy of Music and the Academy of Physical Training. Just after the war, the Mining Academy was transformed into the Mining and Metallurgical Academy. The science of Cracow somehow survived this difficult period of splitting up its higher schools.

Shortly after the changes which took place in 1956, a branch of the Polish Academy of Sciences was called into being in Cracow (1957). An Institute of Nuclear Research was also created in appreciation of the modern development of science.

It would be difficult to mention all the outstanding scientists who work in Cracow. There are many of them, and the research carried on in Cracow is a testimony to the veritable explosion of scientific talent. The technical and exact sciences are in the lead. The Polish Academy of Sciences integrates all the scientific milieux scattered in various higher schools.

In 1964, the scientists of Cracow celebrated a great jubilee: the 600th anniversary of the Jagiellonian University. The jubilee celebrations reminded people of the fine traditions of Poland's oldest university. In connection with its jubilee, the university and other higher schools received several new buildings, which make their research and didactic work much easier.

It would be very difficult to describe the rich and varied cultural panorama of contemporary Cracow. It is not always so easy to assemble facts connected with the cultural life of a city with a population of over half a million. For they are all intertwined, forming a single uniform whole. It will make things easier if we divide them into three groups: literature, art and the theatre.

Cracow's literary traditions go back a long way and it would need a separate work to do full justice to them. After the war, despite the departure of many writers to Warsaw, there was still quite a big literary milieu in Cracow, and the books of the Cracow writers are very popular. From the very beginning there has been a Cracow branch of the Polish Writers' Union. Among the prose writers, mention is due to the writers of historical novels Antoni Gołubiew (d. 1978), and Karol Bunsch (d. 1987); the novelists Stefan Otwinowski, Kornel Filipowicz and the excellent writer of science fiction Stanisław Lem. Drama is represented by the famous writer Sławomir Mrożek, now living in Paris. The poets are represented by Ewa Lipska, Wisława Szymborska, Leszek Elektorowicz and Jerzy Harasymowicz. Literary criticism also developed, to mention Kazimierz Wyka (d. 1975), Henryk Markiewicz and Jan Błoński. The weekly *Życie Literackie* (1951), and the vital publishing firm Wydawnictwo Literackie (1953) are closely associated with the Cracow writers. A number of interesting articles appeared in the columns of *Życie Literackie* which have aroused sometimes heated discussions in the creative milieu. The Cracow writers willingly join cultural events, meeting their readers at authors' soirées. The "Literary Wednesdays" organized every week have gained great popularity. Translators of foreign literature also have their successes (Maciej Słomczyński, Wanda Kragen, Feliks Konopka, Maria Traczewska, Edyta Sicińska, Gabriela Mycielska and Maria Leśniewska).

Numerous periodicals are published in today's Cracow. Besides the dailies *(Dziennik Polski — Gazeta Krakowska, Echo Krakowa)* eagerly read weeklies also appear, which are distributed all over Poland. The illustrated magazine *Przekrój* is very popular. *Tygodnik Powszechny* is important for Polish culture; it is a social and cultural weekly issued by Catholic intellectuals (Jerzy Turowicz, Father Mieczysław Maliński, Marek Skwarnicki, Jacek Woźniakowski, Tadeusz Żychiewicz). Apart from the Wydawnictwo Literackie, there are other publishers active in Cracow: the State Music Publishers (1952), the Cracow branches of Ossolineum, the State Scientific Publishers (PWN), the State Publishing Institute (PIW) and the National Publishing Agency (KAW). There is also the excellent Znak Publishing House, which is a representative of Catholic culture.

A separate place is due to art in the modern culture of Cracow, which after 1956 has passed through all the trends: abstraction, tachisme, pop-art, hyper-realism, etc. The above mentioned artistic trends all found their reflection in the art of Cracow, which by its very nature is all for pluralism.

Directly after the war, a number of architectural designs were carried out in connection with the need for housing estates, including the building done at Nowa Huta. In the years 1949—56, the artistic expression of architecture was determined by socialist realism. Its task was to build flats to suit social transformations of a socialist nature. In architecture efforts were made to link modern architecture with the national traditions. It was not a successful marriage. The result of these efforts were gloomy, monumental blocks of flats, crowned with pseudo-Renaissance parapets.

A sudden change came after 1956. The achievements of modern architecture and town-planning were fully accepted. There was a return to functionalism and simplicity. Tall sky-scrapers began to appear, which gave a strong spatial accent. The professors and graduates of the Architecture Department of the Cracow Technical University made a big contribution to this. In 1961, the building was completed of an interesting block of flats with a hundred balconies, in Retoryka Street, designed by Bohdan Lisowski. The hotel "Cracovia" with the "Kiev" cinema, designed by Witold Cęckiewicz (1964) form a modern complex. The Biprostal building in 18 Stycznia Street is also interesting (Mieczysław Wrześniak, Paweł Czapczyński; 1964). The university buildings built in connection with the jubilee of the university have good architecture: Collegium Paderevianum (Zbigniew Olszakowski, Józef Gołąb), the Collegium Phisicum (Stanisław Juszczyk), the students' hostel Piast (Wojciech Bryzek) and the building of the Agricultural Academy (Stanisław Juszczyk). The new housing estates are marked by their good planning, but the realization and execution of the designs leave much to be desired. The university campus was well designed (the author of the town-planning design was Tomasz Mańkowski).

In the architecture of Cracow in the postwar years, the church at Nowa Huta is worthy of notice for its form (1977). It was designed on the basis of western patterns by W. Pietrzyk.

The architecture of Cracow has generally followed current world trends. Geometric blocks are applied, though the occasional wavy shape can also be seen. It is absolutely linked up with engineering technology, which accounts for its constructive and functional character.

Painting and sculpture underwent dynamic transformations in the postwar years. The situation in painting was not very clear after 1945. Professors from the colourists' group took charge of the Faculty of Painting at the Academy of Fine Arts. They were opposed by young painters of the avant-garde "Group Cracow", and the even younger painters of the "Young Artists' Group", with Tadeusz Kantor, Tadeusz Brzozowski, Jerzy Nowosielski and Kazimierz Mikulski. The exhibition organized by these avant-garde artists in 1948 was a turning point in art. Not long after, the abstract trend was officially split up by the ideology of socialist realism (1949—54). The trend propagated by the authorities was based on Lenin's theory of reflection and propagated fully realistic painting and sculpture. Art was supposed to be understood by everybody. Andrzej Wróblewski's (1927—57) art was in the spirit of socialist realism. Many good artists, in the face of the existing political situation, stopped exhibiting their pictures. But changes in policy and pressure exerted by the arts were stronger than dogmatic recommendations in the end.

After 1956, numerous painters went to Paris, fascinated by the modernity, the variety of current trends there. They brought back new artistic ideas to Poland. Formal pluralism began in Polish art. In Cracow, the "Group Cracow" and the "Young Artists' Group" came to life again and merged to form one group, known under the name of the "Group Cracow". Abstract art became the most attractive for the artists. In that period, the most outstanding artists were Maria Jarema, Adam Marczyński and Jonasz Stern. A separate place should be given to the art of Tadeusz Kantor, who propagated tachisme and did metaphorical paintings, American dripping and action painting. Moreover he also created the "Cricot II" theatre, which has had triumphs also outside Poland. He mostly put on the plays of Witkacy. His "Theatrical Spectacle of the Death of Kantor — A Dead Class" won the appreciation of international critics.

Kazimierz Mikulski paints metaphorical surrealist pictures while Jerzy Nowosielski is fascinated by Byzantine art and paints strange metaphorical landscapes. Surrealistic effects are gained by Józef Szajna, who moved to Warsaw and opened the "Studio" theatre. At present in Cracow, painters still favour the abstract, but with increasing frequency the younger artists are turning to hyperrealism.

The Academy of Fine Arts has educated many excellent sculptors in the postwar years including Jerzy Bandura, Bronisław Chromy and Marian Konieczny. The sculptures of the above mentioned are to be found in many towns all over Poland. The huge commemoration monument on the site of the Battle of Grunwald (J. Bandura) and the Warsaw Nike in Warsaw (M. Konieczny) are particularly noteworthy.

The traditions of artistic handicrafts have been continued by Helena and Stefan Gałkowski who weave beautiful fabrics known widely beyond the frontiers of Poland.

After the war, the Academy of Fine Arts established a Department for the Conservation of Works of Art, which strengthened the staff engaged in the conservation of historic monuments. The Cracow school of conservation was set up by Józef E. Dutkiewicz, a painter, historian of art and conservationist. The achievements of the graduates of the Department of Conservation are

widely appreciated in the world today.

The pupils of Andrzej Stopka are maintaining the good traditions of stage design. International recognition has been won in this field by Kazimierz Wiśniak, Andrzej Majewski and Krystyna Zachwatowicz.

To give a really full picture of the cultural life of Cracow mention is due to theatrical life, which was particularly lively at the beginning of the 1960's. Apart from the theatres that existed from the prewar years, the Stary Theatre and the Słowacki Theatre, new theatres were set up in Nowa Huta (The People's Theatre), and the Rhapsodical Theatre, the Musical Theatre and the Groteska Puppet Theatre. Moreover in the city numerous avant-garde student theatres were active. The only theatre to achieve European fame was the Stary Theatre, which under the direction of Jan Paweł Gawlik (1970—81) began to come to the fore in Polish theatre culture. All the most outstanding stage directors collaborated with this theatre: Konrad Swiniarski, Andrzej Wajda, Jerzy Jarocki and also the stage designers, Kazimierz Wiśniak and Krystyna Zachwatowicz. The ambitious repertoire of the theatre includes the best literary works from the Polish and world classics. Its excellent team of actors (Jerzy Trela, Jan Nowicki, Jerzy Stuhr, Anna Polony and Jerzy Bińczycki) won the hearts of Polish audiences long ago.

A separate chapter in the artistic life of the city is the cabaret "The Cellar At the Sign of the Rams" (*Piwnica pod Baranami*), which has been operating from 1956. It is a specific cultural phenomenon. Under the sponsorship of Piotr Skrzynecki, every Saturday it amuses the audience with excellent literary texts and political satire. The "Cellar" is not only a cabaret but also a place lively with social life, great balls and occasionally other events, too. People of various professions and generations gather round Piotr Skrzynecki to hold passionate discussions on problems of art and contemporary life. From the "Cellar" circle came such celebrities as the singer Ewa Demarczyk, the composers Zygmunt Konieczny and Stanisław Radwan, and the stage designers Kazimierz Wiśniak and Krystyna Zachwatowicz. Andrzej Wajda and the world famous composer Krzysztof Penderecki both have had a special fondness for the "Cellar". To this very day, the "Cellar" still surprises people with its artistic youthfulness and its programmes are marked for the remarkable ingenuity of the texts and their interpretation.

In the last forty years, Cracow has become not only a powerful scholarly and artistic centre, but also a place where Polish and foreign tourists make for. The city, not destroyed by the war, began to attract crowds of tourists from the very beginning. People admired the historic buildings and the works of art collected in the museums. In 1961, the Arras tapestries of Sigismund Augustus came back to Cracow from Canada. The Crown Treasury was brought back earlier (1959). The art of Cracow became famous after the exhibition "The Golden Age of European Towns" organized in Ghent in 1958. Europe began to delight in the treasures of Polish culture kept in Cracow. During the 600th anniversary of the Jagiellonian university, foreign scholars became acquainted with the lasting historical and artistic values of Cracow.

The cultural wealth of Cracow is made up of several hundred historic monuments and hundreds of thousands of works of art kept in the museums and in private collections. This city survived the war together with its treasures that it seemed would be there for always. Unfortunately this is not so. The action of time, the development of industry and motor transport, quickly gave us examples of what they could do to our treasures. The historic buildings began to slowly crumble. Emergency conservation measures were no longer enough to save them. At last, the central authorities began to take an interest in what was happening to the architectural heritage of Cracow. Specialized enterprises were called into being to work on conservation. The government resolutions of 1961, 1967 and 1974 formulated a long-term plan for the restoration of old Cracow. But these were only half-measures, although the state treasury allotted five hundred million zlotys annually for this purpose.

The year 1978 marked a turning point in the restoration of Cracow. By a decision of international experts, UNESCO put Cracow on the list of places representing the world's cultural heritage. So it became not only a matter for the Polish nation to settle. In the justification of the decision we read of the exceptional historical and cultural values of Cracow, as one of the artistic complexes of Europe most worthy of attention. The final formulation of UNESCO says that Cracow passes on to coming generations a unique collection of monuments to the culture of past centuries — outstanding works of art and architecture. Just after this historic fact, the Praesidium of the All-Poland Committee of the National Unity Front met in Cracow at the end of September and called into being a Civic Committee for the Restoration of the Historic Monuments of Cracow. An appeal to the whole nation reads: "Not one of us should be lacking in the alliance of Polish hearts and hands that is being set up now. The restoration of Cracow should be carried out with the cooperation of the whole nation. Concern for the preservation of invaluable testimonies to national traditions is an expression of respect for our origin, an essential part of true patriotism." This appeal was answered by everybody who still loved the ancient Cracow. A fund for the Restoration of Cracow was set up. Generous contributions came in from all over the world. At the same time, after years of neglect, systematic work was started on the restoration of Cracow. Not only outstanding historic buildings are conserved, everything that gives the city its unique atmosphere and charm is subject to conservation and renewal. The municipal landscape of Cracow is made up of great and small things, like the little streets, the picturesque lanes, the courtyards, the old gates into the courtyards and beautiful vestibules. Every detail is being saved, and older elements are being discovered in the process. The restored buildings will serve generations to come. The saving of the former capital of Poland has become the duty of the whole nation.

The autumn of 1978 brought one more historical event, this time in keeping with the millennium of the Polish state. This made Cracow famous all over the world. On 16 October after the conclusion of the conclave of cardinals, Proto-Deacon Porcile Felici proclaimed *urbi et orbi* that the head of the Church elected by the College of Cardinals, was Archbishop of Cracow Karol Wojtyła, who had taken the name John Paul II.

Pope John Paul II grew up in the intellectual atmosphere of Cracow, with its university, scholars and intellectuals. It was in Cracow that he studied and in Cracow that he experienced the hardships of physical labour during the Nazi occupation. In Cracow, he also performed as an actor in the underground Rhapsody Theatre, run by Mieczysław Kotlarczyk. He was deeply involved in the unique atmosphere of Cracow. His election was received with incredulity, although the Cracovians well knew his importance in the Catholic Church. The election of Cardinal Wojtyła as Pope became an event widely commented in the whole world. The first non-Italian Pope for 455 years, a Slav, a Pole. This was a possibility that could not be envisaged, even in the boldest assumptions, although for years it had been spoken of repeatedly but with a wide margin of disbelief. Today in Cracow we call back the memory of a figure in a black cassock with a cross on his breast, full of peace, but at the same time friendly and open.

The essential feature of this great man has been his authentic love and respect for the dignity of man. He made his faithful realize this on every occasion. This eminent intellectual, outstanding expert on theological and moral problems, a warm and cheerful person of amazing simplicity — well understands the spirit suffusing his beloved Cathedral on Wawel Hill. He has expressed this more than once. He wrote: "There emerges in the cathedral, as a living truth, the whole of our great thousand-year-old traditions of Christianity and, at the same time, Polish traditions... Here, in Cracow Cathedral, within its venerable walls, there is the past of Poland, that most magnificent, most honourable, truly good, worth imitating and worthy of eternal memory." He loves Wawel and Cracow, which shaped his uncommon personality. He has sometimes identified Cracow with Poland, equating the two notions: "Poland," he said, "is a thousand years of history. Poland is Wawel Hill, this Cathedral, these royal tombs. Poland is an immense quantity of victories and suffering."

An eastern view of the Wawel Castle

A view of the Wawel Castle from the
Vistula

Interior of the Rotunda
of the Blessed Virgin Mary
(of SS. Felix and Adauctus),
dating from c. 1000

A Romanesque window in the
Rotunda of the Blessed Virgin
Mary

Capital with strapped
ornaments dating from the
first quarter of the 11th
century

Romanesque Church of
St. Andrew, late 11th
century

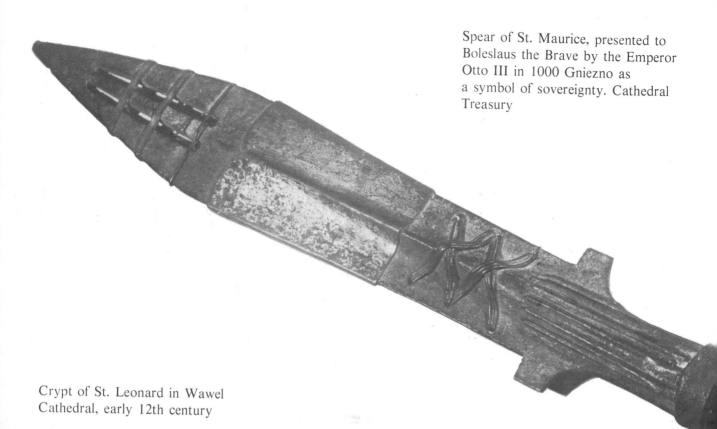

Spear of St. Maurice, presented to Boleslaus the Brave by the Emperor Otto III in 1000 Gniezno as a symbol of sovereignty. Cathedral Treasury

Crypt of St. Leonard in Wawel Cathedral, early 12th century

Attributes of the Four
Evangelists from
Predicationes, late
8th century

Christ Enthroned,
miniature from the Gospel
Book of Emmeram, early
12th century. Library of the
Cracow Chapter

Crosses made from ducal diadems, mid-13th century.
Cathedral Treasury

Saracene casket, mid-12th century. Cathedral Treasury

Mitre of St. Stanislaus, mid-13th century.
Cathedral Treasury

Sandomierz Tower in the Wawel Castle

Senators' Tower and old walls of the Wawel Castle

A south-eastern view of the Gothic
Wawel Cathedral, 1320—64

Barbican, 1498—99

Florian's Gate and old city walls, after 1300

Church of the Blessed Virgin Mary, 14th—15th centuries

A view of the presbytery of
the Church of the BVM with
the Church of St. Barbara,
14th—15th centuries,
in the foreground

The Dormition in the High altar
of the Church of the BVM,
1477—89

A view of the Main Market Place

Main Market Place and the townhall tower, 1383—1444

Church of the Corpus Christi,
1340—1405

Former townhall in Kazimierz
(now Ethnographic Museum),
15th—19th centuries

Old Synagogue
at Kazimierz, early
16th century

Jewish cemetery
at Kazimierz

Church of St. Catherine, 2nd
half of the 14th century

Portal in the southern vestibule
in the Church of St. Catherine,
c. 1400

Church of the Holy Cross,
14th century

Church of St. Barbara, 14th—
15th centuries

Church of Franciscan Fathers,
13th—15th centuries

Presbytery of the Franciscan
Church with Xawery
Dunikowski's monument to
Józef Dietl, mayor of Cracow,
in the foreground, 1936

Church of St. Mark, 13th—
15th centuries

Franciscan monastery, 14th
century

Front gable of the Wawel
Cathedral, c. 1364

Detail of the main
wrought iron door of Wawel
Cathedral with initials
of King Casimir the Great,
c. 1364

Sandomierz Crown, probably of
Casimir the Great, early 14th
century

Sarcophagus of Casimir
the Great in Wawel Cathedral,
1370—80

Arcaded courtyard of the Wawel
Castle, 1507—36

Bay window of the Collegium
Maius, early 15th century

Courtyard of the Collegium
Maius, after 1493

Stove tile with the Polish Eagle
from the Wawel Castle, early
16th century

Banners of the Teutonic Knights
captured in the Battle of Grunwald in
1410, from the Wawel Castle

Chamber in the Hen's Foot Tower in the
Wawel Castle

Holy Trinity Triptych in
Wawel Cathedral

Representation of
St. Eustace hunting from
the Holy Trinity Triptych

Gothic presbytery with
a view of the high altar
in Wawel Cathedral,
mid-17th century

Dome of the Sigismund Chapel,
1519—33, designed by
Bartolommeo Berrecci

Sigismund Chapel, mausoleum
of the last Jagiellon kings,
Sigismund the Old and
Sigismund Augustus, c. 1573

Silver altar piece in the
Sigismund Chapel, 1538

Cover of the prayerbook of
Anna the Jagiellon, 1582.
Jagiellonian Library

Cloth Hall in the Main Market Place, 1556—59, converted by Tomasz Pryliński in 1875—79

Polish parapet with mascarons by Santi Gucci adorning Cloth Hall, c. 1559

Renaissance loggia of the Cloth Hall

Three volumes of the Gradual of John Albert on a table in the library of the Cracow Chapter at Wawel

Miniature with a representation of the Holy Trinity in the Gradual of John Albert. Library of the Cracow Chapter

Miniature showing a tailor's shop from the *Behem Codex*, after 1505

Detail of a page from the Gospel Book of Bishop Tomicki, 1533—34. Library of the Cracow Chapter

Sigismund Bell endowed by
King Sigismund the Old, 1520,
the work of the bellfounder
Hans Beham. Wawel Cathedral

Sepulchral sculpture of Bishop
Andrzej Zebrzydowski, 1562—
62, the work of Jan Michałowicz
of Urzędów. Wawel Cathedral

Details of the tomb of Ladislaus
Jagiello showing the king's
head, 1st quarter of the 15th
century. Wawel Cathedral

Tomb of King Casimir the Jagiellon, 1492, by Wit Stwosz. Wawel Cathedral

Detail of Casimir the Jegiellon's head

Reliquary for the head of St. Florian (formerly St. Stanislaus), 2nd quarter of the 15th century. Cathedral Treasury

Reliquary for the head of St. Stanislaus, 1504, by the goldsmith Marcin Marciniec

Chasuble of Bishop Jan Kmita, c. 1504. Cathedral Treasury

Detail of the chasuble of Jan Kmita
showing the assasination of Bishop
Stanislaus Szczepanowski

Title page of *Chronica Polonorum* by
Maciej of Miechów, published in
Cracow in 1521

Arras with the initials of Sigismund
Augustus, mid-16th century

Senators' Hall with Arrases from the
series *The Flood,* mid-16th century.
Wawel Castle

Arras with the coats-of-arms of Poland
and Lithuania, mid-16th century

Vaulting coffered ceiling of the Senators'
Hall in Wawel Castle, c. 1535

Birds' Chamber in Wawel Castle,
c. 1600

Church of St. Peter with its front dating from 1622—30 designed by Giovanni Trevano

Dutch Chamber in the Wawel Castle representing interior design of the Vasa period, 17th century

Crypt with the coffins of the Vasa kings in Wawel Cathedral

Mausoleum or Shrine of St. Stanislaus in Wawel Cathedral, 1628—30, designed by Giovanni Trevano

Silver coffin from the shrine of St. Stanislaus, 1669—71, the work of Peter von der Rennen

Paulite Church and Monastery on the Rock (na Skałce), 1733—51, designed by Anton G. Müntzer and Antonio Solari

Interior of the Church of St. Anne, 1689—1703, designed by Tylman of Gameren, with stucco work by Balthasar

The Słowacki Theatre, 1893, designed by Jan Zawiejski

Auditorium of the Słowacki Theatre

Collegium Novum of the
Jagiellonian University, 1887,
designed by Feliks Księżarski

Academy of Fine Arts, 1880,
designed by Maciej Moraczewski

PROJ. S. WYSPIAŃSKI.
WYKONAŁ
KRAKOWSKI ZAKŁAD WITRAŻÓW S. G. ŻELEŃSKI.

Stained-glass window in the Church of the BVM,
1889—91, by Stanisław Wyspiański and Józef Mehoffer

Sarcophagus of Stanisław Wyspiański
in the crypt of famous Poles in the
Church on the Rock

The Stary (Old) Theatre, 1905,
designed by Tadeusz Stryjeński
and Franciszek Mączyński,
with the frieze
by Jozef Gardecki

Society of the Friends of Fine
Arts, 1901, with its front
designed by Franciszek Mączyński

INDEX OF NAMES